HIDING
IN PLAIN SIGHT

Confessions of an Angel Messenger

LISA ANN

Disclaimer Notice

DEDICATIONS

To all my woo woo friends that receive and relay messages for me for many years now, thank you for listening to the call from spirit.

Cathy G., never question that your presence in other lives is profound. You have seen me at my worst two times now. I now dub thee a saint. Thank you for your continued support and always agreeing to solving world problems with me over sushi.

Agent 007., I hope you never get bored of me telling you how much of an angel you are. Thank you for being there for me when I couldn't be there for myself for a while.

Mom & Steve, you will never fully understand how much your contribution saved me and how spirit used you in that endeavor. Thank you for listening.

To Houdini, I am grateful for our connection. Thank you for choosing me. I look forward to being your teacher, and witnessing the magic you will bring into this world.

To Grandpa, Grandma & G. Aunt – I know what you have done to help me, and I am forever grateful. Thank you for making us all laugh.

TABLE OF CONTENTS

PREFACE

R*eally, spirit?*
Really?

No, I don't want to move—especially not back to the place that broke me. Can you show me any other options? Can you lead me to the pile of resources and all this great stuff you have given to me in messages?

Here I am, a practicing psychic medium, and I can't seem to help myself. Doesn't this seem a bit contradictory and unfair, or is it just me? I do so much for others and yet I can't even see the clear decisions to aid my own life. What's up with that?

I want to hide for a bit, and catch my breath, but there is no time. I need bricks to rebuild. Moreover, I don't want to come under scrutiny for my decisions over the past few years.

All this is coming just as I'd finally felt like I was striking a balance in my new life in North Carolina. I moved here after my divorce was finalized, and I sold everything I owned. I'd taken a break from my job as a real estate agent and cut off most of my friends. I felt I could only trust a select few. I needed to breathe and move away from the sneers, the gossip, and the expectations of friends and family. I had no smile to give anyone anymore. I was not the same happy-go-lucky person, and I needed to refill the empty shell I had become.

In North Carolina, I've found my footing and my smile again. I've made friends and taken classes that were of interest to me in metaphysics. I've learned to meditate and calm my forever-racing mind. I've started getting words, pictures, and thoughts during these meditations and started writing them down. I've taken more classes in psychic development, oracle card reading, intuitiveness, and mediumship, just to name a few. I've even studied at the Arthur Findlay College of spiritualism and psychic sciences in England, which I fondly call Hogwarts. I've realized that these were experiences that have always been a part of me! They were innate gifts that I have always had and unknowingly used. The classes showed me how to work with them. As time moved on, I felt settled enough to sell real estate in North Carolina as well as do readings for others on the side. I even started my own woo-woo practice group with my new friends to try out new skills we wanted to explore.

And then COVID came along, and the world came to a screeching halt. My mental state and my money reserves have started to dwindle. I can feel another change for me is on the horizon. I am different now. Stronger and yet still fragile in some ways. I'd just gotten on my feet in North Carolina when the rug seemed to have been pulled out from under me with all this. I was stubborn and standing on the last remaining thread of my safety net. Then it was gone.

The only two choices I see are to stay in North Carolina, live under a bridge, and save face. Or move back to Florida, broke and homeless, where a lot of people know me. Moving back, I would have my career to get me up and running again—but I'd be embarrassed as hell. I have bragging rights, doing what most others just talk about. I picked up my life and moved. I originally left Florida after my divorce with my pride, a game plan, and a small amount of financial padding from selling my house. Moving back is not the same. Great options, eh? Seriously, I question at times if the bridge is the better choice.

Even though I have a direct line to my spirit guides, I feel left out in the cold. If there are other options for me, I don't know what they are. The only option I feel I have is to move back to Florida. Hands down, I will struggle along the way. I will be forced to rebuild myself in front of some gloating adversaries.

Spirit, where is my cloak of invisibility while I do this? Spirit gave me the drop-in message that I will have some privacy and anonymity for my gifts ... for now. The rest, not so much. It just wouldn't be as bad as I think it will be. I am not so sure about that.

I have been gone from Florida for a few years now, and I'm not the same person as I was when I left. I want to do more with my gifts, but the people in my world in Florida are not nearly as accepting as they are in North Carolina. Whenever I would travel back to Florida, I was extremely cautious of who I spent time with, where I went, and who I spoke to. I didn't talk about my psychic/mediumship gifts at all. I put on the hat of the person I used to be before I moved and thought they expected me to be. I hid from the friends I stopped talking to without giving an explanation as to why.

I still have to care what others think. I can't very well talk to all my past real estate clients and tell them what I can do or the hardships I have endured. They will change my name in their phones to "squirrely/unstable" and never call me again. I have way too many bills to pay. Despite the smile I might have on my face, I also need to keep my energy high. Being positive and grateful helps me to receive messages during readings for people who have no idea what is going on with me. I cannot blur the lines between their life messages and my own.

I know from the many channeled readings I've done for myself that there are many events to come, specifically new love, and the return of someone from my past. Right now, I just need to get my footing with a solid foundation again while I hide in plain sight.

I have no choice but to face all that I have managed to avoid— well, most of it. Spirit said no more hiding with most things. The next leg of my journey will be to move back and rebuild myself from scratch—in front of my family and now two ex-husbands—all while acting like everything is OK.

With my tail between my legs, I have to move. For now, I still have to hide what I can do. Funny, I used to have a junior detective badge for snooping and now I am a secret agent for spirit in hiding.

Here we go!

PROLOGUE

T*hen* ...

My second marriage did a number on me, mentally and emotionally. We had done this dance for years; six months on and six months off. The patterns and habits kept repeating themselves year after year. As I noticed them more and more, I knew what stage we were in and what to expect next. Then I came across the Portia Nelson story called Autobiography in Five Short Chapters.

Chapter 1

I walk down the street.

There is a deep hole in the sidewalk.

I fall in. I am lost.

It isn't my fault.

It takes forever to find a way out.

Chapter 2

I walk down the same street.

There is a deep hole in the sidewalk.

I pretend I don't see it. I fall in again.

I can't believe I am in this same place.

But it isn't my fault.

It still takes a long time to get out.

Chapter 3

I walk down the same street.

There is a deep hole in the sidewalk.

I see it there.

I still fall in. It's a habit, but my eyes are open.

I know where I am.

It was my fault.

I get out immediately.

Chapter 4

I walk down the street.

There is a deep hole in the sidewalk.

I walk around it.

Chapter 5

I walk down another street.

Profound, isn't it? It certainly summed up what I was going through in my life for sure!

Although I was consumed with finding evidence of the indiscretions that I just knew were going on under my nose, I was hearing comments in my thoughts that weren't mine. My thoughts were on my side—egging me along to dig and find out anything to justify the perpetually uneasy gut feeling I had in the pit of my stomach. Staring into my ex's eyes after another confrontation of evidence I literally heard the word LIAR in my head as he once again gave excuses. That voice was not mine! It was true, but not mine!

Since talking wasn't working, I wrote a last-ditch letter to explain my feelings to him. My fingers flew, writing a way-too-nice statement that I didn't feel would have been my choice of words. The letter didn't work. After that, I had nothing left. I wanted my marriage to work but knew in my heart that it wasn't going to. Too much damage was done, and it was obvious to me I was the only

one trying.

One morning after that, I sat at the end of the driveway saying my prayers out loud through tears. The statement that ran through my head was: *When the fear of change is less than the fear of staying the same, it is time to move on.* That made so much sense to me at that moment. I finally said, *God, I surrender. Please get me out of this. I don't want to ever feel like this again. I will do whatever you need me to do.* The proverbial white flag was waved, and I was ready to move on—hopefully for good this time.

One year after we pledged to be together, I was in the attorney's office filing the paperwork I needed to move on. I started educating myself via books and online material of words and phrases told to me during psychic and intuitive readings I was getting during my relationship. This helped me realize that others had gone through this mental hell and how they got out of it. The shame I felt was eased a bit knowing I wasn't alone.

I packed my belongings and moved to North Carolina to heal. I discovered and developed my own psychic and mediumistic abilities, made new friends and got established. I had finally found myself.

Along came COVID, the draining of my bank account and the need to move back to Florida. Sink or swim. The only two choices I had. Once again, starting over from square one. UGH.

I want to continue to write, but only happy stories! No more wild "you can't make this stuff up" stories anymore, spirit!

When will this all end?

1

LIFE TOLD THROUGH MUSIC

Hello, my name is Lisa and I love music. Music is a type of drug to me. It enhances my mood, sets the ambience, or digs up a memory. I liken it to the soundtrack of my life.

Music has been the soundtrack of significant events in my life for as long as I can remember. When I arrived home and my mom had "elevator music" on, I knew she was in a good mood! Then, there was this song I remember and, to this day, when I hear it, I am instantly teleported back to the airport where we were seeing someone off when I was still little. The next song of significance came around the time I had my appendix taken out. Why on earth would a seven-year-old girl have a song to go along with the removal of an emergency appendectomy? Because I had to share a hospital room with a teenager. She had friends visiting and that was the song on the radio when they talked to me. Coincidentally, I remember trying to have an "*I'm as cool as you*" conversation with them, said the word "*damn*," and caught the glances of amused eyes between them.

Then there was the first song I was able to buy by myself—"Another One Bites the Dust." Over and over, I would play that song.

Fast forward to those "dreamy, googly-eyed teenage years" when every profound love song that came on was attached to the latest crush. *sigh* I spent hours and hours trying to capture the latest Journey title I liked so I could listen any time I wanted.

There was the first kiss song. The make-out song. The first breakup song. Of course, every amazing memory and "first" had a song attached to it. I can't remember every song by name but when I hear it, I instantly recall a memory.

I have learned through the years that some people are all about words, some about acoustics and some the beat. I am a beat person. It took me a while to figure that out. The beats just made me feel a certain way. It also explained why someone did not like the same songs as I did.

Do not get me started on air-drum solos. DISCLAIMER: No lie, if you see me looking like Animal from *The Muppets* in a car thrashing around all wide-eyed and crazy acting, just nod toward me—for I am undoubtedly performing the air-drum solo to Phil Collins's "In the Air Tonight." No joke! It is just what I do! If you know the song, you know the part I am talking about. I have friends trained to let me know whatever station it is playing on. No matter what, my car volume goes all the way up and my imaginary "drumsticks" appear ready for the drum solo. EVERY-SINGLE-TIME.

Anyway, I have song assignments that are attached to people, places, and events in my life even to this day. I cannot remember why I walked into the next room sometimes, but I can tell you about a song, where I was, and who was with me. Some songs are like a time machine.

I realized that being a beat and melody person, I just liked the song but never listened to the words. I just liked how I felt or the memory it evoked and just blindly sang along to whatever words I thought they were singing.

I did learn a very valuable lesson about not paying attention to words or a song's meaning years ago.

In middle school health class, my teacher, Ms. Mucci, started out the semester with sex education. A popular song out at the time was "The Stroke" by Billy Squire. She opened the discussion by asking the class what we thought the song was about. I may or may not have adamantly raised my hand to answer the music question. *Ms. Mucci, it's about a boat ride!*

See, I had pictured in my mind George Washington-ish men in white wigs and red jackets lined up in rowboats while the man directing them would yell *STROKE! STROKE! STROKE!* Obviously, I was very naive. What did I know?

Oh, if you could have seen the smirk on her face and then heard the giggles in the room. No doubt I was the topic of laughter in the teachers' lounge that day. Lessoned learned, or so I thought.

So fast forward to the upheavals of life and the unbeknownst song attachments that went along with those moments. I truly just like music but holy cow, when they come on, I become some sort of Wikipedia master with all the information about them as it pertains to my life. After all, music is the soundtrack to the events of my life.

A lot of times I don't know why I like a song let alone what the hell I'm singing. Again, for me it's about the beat. I would say I do not really pay attention to the lyrics about 95 percent of the time. Then there is the 5 percent that spirit will nudge me and say *AHEM!* So, I will pause and actually hear what I'm singing about. Honestly, there are words and phrases, and a lot of other not-so-nice things I am just singing along with conviction, like they were my words, but I never noticed before.

I have around eighteen thousand songs on my computer. I am sure there are duplicates from when I transferred them to new computers. My playlists are broken down into groups. Whatever the most appropriate soundtrack for the event is what I turn on. Singing is a great way to elevate your spirit and raise your vibration—something I did not know until recently. *Fa-la-la-la-laaaaa!*

What has been interesting to me of late is actually listening to the words of old songs that were popping up. Song after song, I am suddenly hearing what I have been singing about.

BOOM! My mind was blown! Most songs are a story put to music and I had interest in them for the beat and melody, not for what they were saying. Suddenly I am listening to what a lot of the songs are about!

I found it profound that my soul liked these songs because of what was going on in my life at the moment. I did not even realize it. Song lyrics were suddenly illuminated. So many songs about strength and resilience but also heartbreak and sorrow. Seriously, the majority of them have shocked me into saying, *Holy cow, I had no idea*!

Recently I realized that my playlists and songs were crooning over issues and evoking memories of my past. They no longer belonged in my future. It has been on my to-do list to update my playlists and add new songs I like. So why am I suddenly aware of all of this? Spirit was bringing this to my attention to change it. *It is time!* My playlists are well overdue to be updated so I can sing about what is going on in my life now. Out with the old and in with the new!

These older songs will always be part of my history, but they are not a part of my future. I swear it is like spirit has made me so aware of what songs I am singing to lately that I cannot ignore it anymore. Maybe they will be placed back in rotation way down the line, but for now they have to go! That is not to say that I will not belt out an old favorite at karaoke or sing in the car if an "oldie" comes on.

I truly think it was spirit, reminding me that it was time for new songs to go along with all the new (and improved) memories. Basically, it was time for a new soundtrack to go along with my new and improved life.

What you listen to and feed your mind makes a difference. I see how this applied to my music choices. So, the new playlist project has moved to the top of my to-do list. Rest assured though, no matter what, when "In the Air Tonight" comes on, those imaginary drumsticks will always be pulled out of my back pocket for an impromptu drum solo.

Dear Reader,

What you listen to, what you read, and what you are drawn to listen to is often a sign. If you are always listening to negativity and question why things are negative in your life, it could be a sign. Unhealed areas show up in unsuspecting ways!

2

So, I Did a Thing, North Carolina

I stopped writing and now I'm back! I actually quit writing for almost a year. Writing and journaling have been my go-to vice to get thoughts out of my mind and off my chest. It is also to have a benchmark to look back on. Well, OK, I stopped. Just cold turkey stopped.

I just felt done! Finished. I had ideas to write about and kept an ongoing list for when I felt up to it again. Honestly though, I lost the desire. I couldn't find the goofy magical spin I normally did.

What happened? Everything. Nothing. I didn't know, actually. There really wasn't just one catalyst. My goal in writing is first and foremost for personal therapy. I needed to shine a light using humor to get through tough situations, like my divorce. I also was sorting out my thoughts about all the amazing spiritual unfolding I was having. My goal was that by writing and sharing it, it might help others look at their life through new eyes. By example, maybe someone else would also realize that they don't have to have control over everything. Yes, there are lessons to be learned. I just hoped to show myself and others through reflection that it will all be fine.

Oh, it is so damn easy to say all that and then something tweaks and your perspective changes.

Was life all hunky-dory? Not for me. Frankly, my optimistic attitude could not find its way out of a paper bag, and I lost my mojo. So, I gave myself a self-imposed break.

"HELLO, MY NAME IS LISA AND IT'S BEEN ELEVEN MONTHS SINCE I WROTE A BLOG ENTRY."

(The crowd cheers, HI, LISA! WE MISSED YOU!)

I have a friend who I call Agent 007. We have been friends for many years since both of our kids were younger. She and I bought Apple watches a few years ago so we could be more hands-free. Now that we can talk to each other through our watches, I nicknamed her Agent 007, and I am Agent 008.

She was even asking why I wasn't writing any longer. I was honest and told her I just wasn't feeling it. There was no other explanation I could give to explain it. Even I didn't understand.

Was there stuff going on? Of course! Was I finding the lessons and the humor in my circumstances? Of course not! Well, most of it at least. I just didn't write about anything. Not even for myself personally.

Life got really rough for me. I have always prided myself on not being in this wonky of a position as I am mostly a glass-half-full kind of gal. But I was having the mother-of-all-temper tantrums over a few things and I-SHUT-DOWN. The warning label on my forehead said in big, bold letters: GO HIDE.

What pray-tell happened to get me to such a point of no return for almost a year? Frankly, nothing that would make sense to anyone else really. The best way to paraphrase it was that I was angry.

My vacation down fun-and-easy street after the divorce was over. Although I had done some work already, surprise, surprise, there was more to do. The piper had now come a calling'. I had more shadow work to do and deep-seated things to let go of.

What is shadow work? It is the hurt, resentment, and wounds we all have and think we keep well hidden. This trauma affects who we are and why we act the way we do. Shadow work requires you to really dig deep, be accountable for your actions to examine, deal with, and forgive yourself for not knowing it could or should be different.

Some of my shadow work involved not being a people pleaser, not giving 110 percent and expecting (and believing) I only deserved 5 percent in return. This brought up more self-worth issues to address. Some other shadow sides of me are that my life and actions were sacrificial in nature for the good of others—almost like a penance to pay. I had to dig back into my childhood—the root of where it all began—and really strip down to the bare bones of the actions of others, their wounding and how hurt people hurt people. I will give you a hearty *you're welcome* for not boring you with the details of what this round of work entailed for me. After all, you have your own Band-Aids to rip off and deep-seated issues to deal with once you do the work. I will let you know that it's not as scary as you think. It just makes you really do some digging. Once your eyes are opened to it all, you get strength in your spine you weren't expecting.

So back to why I stopped writing. Let's see, for starters there was an abrupt stop to my jaunting around. Like others, I suddenly felt grounded and in solitary confinement because of COVID. Then, like many others in the world, my financial resources dried up fast because of it. There were things that didn't happen as I thought they were going to, when I wanted them to. Add to that a massive dose of excessive pride, ego issues, and an unwillingness to ask for help, not only physically but mentally. I needed to make major decisions and like everyone else, my life came to a screeching halt. You get the picture.

Again, you're welcome.

So, I just threw my hands up in the air and said, I AM DONE. NO MORE. I just couldn't be optimistic, happy and find humor in life when mine was (for me) in shambles.

In the past when I threw my hands up in the air and surrendered, things still moved, and I just took my hands off the wheel. This time? NOPE. I had to just sit there like the rest of the world, and it was not fun at all!

Mind you, again in the middle of a plague, my family and close friends were healthy. The crisis that plagued many never made it to my doorstep. Honestly, I didn't feel I deserved to whine considering what everyone else was going through. I was so damn lucky and yet couldn't see it for a while.

I had a hard time feeling guilty if I did complain or even think of asking for help when so many others had it a million times worse.

I have been going back and reading all the messages I received channeling for myself and from the others in my woo-woo group of talented friends who can also receive messages, looking for any clues. When was all this great stuff going to come to me that was promised? What have I done wrong that it has not come to me yet? Have I not done enough shadow work or not met some unspoken expectation? Will someone in the spirit world please answer me?

Trust me, that was the short litany of what stress I felt. When everyone around and in the world was also grabbing for a life vest, who do I ask for help from? I have always been the helper, and yet I couldn't help others let alone even ask for myself. I turned inward, closed myself off to everyone and everything. The hole I put myself in was closing in more each day and was very, very dark.

So, I stayed home and ate my feelings while I tried to figure things out like everyone else through COVID. Doing so chiseled away at my self-esteem in the process, but I seriously couldn't have cared less. The biggest decision I was capable of making was what stretchy PJs I going to wear for the day and what wig I would wear for the next Zoom meeting. I prayed every morning but even that was short: "Thank you, God. Keep the kids and baby safe, AMEN."

I put on a great face for the Zoom calls I participated in. My heart was deflated though. I was void of hope and optimism in my own life. The dullness and life force I finally built back up after my divorce was fading faster than I cared to admit.

What can I say? I am human. I put on my fake smile and waited for the world to pass me by. I had jumped off the hope train into a very dark hole. No one knew I was there.

Did my attitude fix anything? Nope! In fact, being void of hope, I kept sinking deeper and deeper. I won't mention how deep or bad it actually had gotten.

I think this was the second-biggest tantrum I have ever had. The last one was being miserable in my marriage of only one year and out of options for how to fix it. I agreed to take my hands off the wheel of this unsatisfying disaster of a marriage and let my angels take over—whatever that meant. The answers and decisions just started coming forth to me and I suddenly felt a sense of calm that everything was going to be fine. Life moved on.

This time? Nope! I needed spirit to throw me a bone. A crumb. A hint, or a freaking life vest! I just refused to back down on this one! I am sure spirit tried to help. Honestly if it didn't look like I thought it should, well, then for me help simply wasn't there. It was my way or the highway. Which by the way, didn't work.

Did it stop drop-in messages from my spirit guides through my friends? Nope! My amazing group of talented psychics and medium friends in my woo-woo group would receive a message meant for me during their own meditation. They would call or text me to explain what the message was as they interpreted it. They never knew the true depth of my frustration. Did I accept those messages? Nope! If it wasn't a clear, black-and-white go-left-at-the-stop-sign kind of message, I would disregard it. I was done with all the guessing games. Being as stubborn as I was, it was like I said, *not good enough, spirit!*

Try again! It was a massive battle of wills, I tell you. Lil' ole me versus angels, my grandparents and great-aunt in the spirit world.

Did spirit make it any easier for me? Oh, hell no! I was grappling with many decisions and choices with unclear answers. I asked about everything and got nothing I quantified as an answer. It was like I was going kicking and screaming through a tunnel to where they needed me to go but wouldn't tell me.

I had a serious case of analysis paralysis. Ever get like that? I used to be a fast, decisive decision-maker and now I can't move or make any decisions. The visual was that I was at the top of an hourglass being squeezed through the neck, hoping to fall into the bottom section where there was space and fresh air. I couldn't move so they made me. Think of a parent holding the hand of a kicking and unruly toddler escorting them out of a store. That was me.

I felt punished. For what? I don't know. I did what they nudged me to do. I got out of a toxic relationship, moved three states away from everything I knew, settled down in a new area, found my woo-woo powers and thought I was doing good in the world!

There were pros and cons to every decision I needed to make, and none were a clear choice to me. To add insult to injury I saw people around me just living-the-life on social media who didn't live by me. Oh, that irked me to no end. You know the ones I'm talking about; they do all sorts of bad things, have a horrible moral compass, and yet are rewarded with new fun beginnings over and over again. OK, let me move on here. I'm not getting on that soapbox. I will never get off it! Let's just say that a lot of things simply didn't seem fair.

In one breath I was very grateful that my sphere was healthy and not dealing with what was going on in the world and in the next yelling: What the hell did I ever do to you, spirit?

I want to stress that I was forced to make decisions that I didn't want to make. COVID and a world lockdown didn't give me many options. I thought North Carolina was going to be my forever home. Yet to get back on my feet having finally run out of resources, I felt no other choice but to move back to the place that broke me—except this time—BROKE has hell. I had a pocketful of pride and no money in my wallet. I never knew this was part of the journey. There was no clear understanding of why this was happening.

When you go through an awakening and do shadow work it can feel frustrating. Sometimes the fear of making ANY choice for fear of it being wrong is paralyzing. I just couldn't handle any more bad situations should I make the wrong decision. Compounding everything going on only magnified more needs for myself that I didn't want to admit I needed.

Hello, my name is Lisa. Pride and ego are my armor, and stubbornness is my game.

Did that stop spirit from putting blessings in my path? Absolutely not. Unexpected refunds were given to me. I would have small pockets of money sent to me out of the blue. Offers of places to sleep and a hot meal were put in my path. I didn't have to sleep in my car as I fought off what seemed my only option of moving back to Florida.

I had messages given to me about this and many dreams. Many random things were put in my path here and there as I was told that there would be. I was told that they would appear at the "right time." UGH! Let me stress this was not my timing. But alas, they did show up. I didn't recognize any of this at the time but only when I look back did I realize what was going on.

If you know me, you know that I never ask for help. It is not in my wheelhouse. What has been told to me for the last few years is, "Ask for help. Your friends will help you." I just couldn't bring myself to ask. If it wasn't offered freely without me asking for it, I just didn't ask.

Nothing happened overnight but help did appear. Baby steps forward started happening.

I was given things out of the blue when I needed them. This was oh so harshly humbling to me.

I help others! They aren't supposed to help me!

Well, I'm here to tell you they did.

Some standout moments were: My good friend and her entire family showed up to move my stuff out of my place and into a storage container when I finally decided I had to move back to Florida. They offered. I didn't ask. I will tell you that I had no choice but to say yes. I was physically, emotionally, and mentally unable. On top of that, I was so over-tired, over-stressed, and so far gone, a massive personal shutdown was imminent. In fact, the day before, I called my friend, heaving sobs and bawling. I told her she was in charge. I had no strength or energy to make any decisions and she needed to play the best game of Tetris she had ever played with my stuff, fitting it into a pod for storage that I thought would be too small.

She and her family showed up with happy compassionate smiles, warm hugs, a box of pizza, and were angels and saints to me. They then put a roof over my head and a safe place to stay for a few days so I could calm down after moving out of my apartment but before I got on the road.

I had another friend who let me camp out with her for a few days while I was deciding my next steps. She was another angel put in my path offering me help without me asking for it.

Money was spontaneously gifted to me to help here and there with no explanation. To be very transparent here, some were from places I could only call a gift from my grandparents on the other side. (Seriously!)

When I finally settled down after moving back to Florida, I was doing more readings again, and monetary tips were gifted to me. Loans were offered if I needed them.

I was barely one or two steps back from the edge of the black hole of despair I was in, and my head was (barely) above water. I knew there were still more changes to come. I still failed to understand it all. I was smiling on the outside but certainly not on the inside.

Just so you know, spirit doesn't care if your bills are late or not. I find this *ha-larious!* My grandparents are rolling over in their graves. Grandpa was a stickler for paying bills on time as am I! Alas, some things had to go by the wayside during this transition. I know I am not alone, and many others were in the same situation. This was a very hard pill for me to swallow.

Was I a singled-out case in any of this? Oh, HELL-NO! Hello! There was this plague going around! To me though, I felt I was being singled out. My ego, pride and credit score were taking a massive beating!

Back in Florida, let me just say Agent 007 and my parents also came through with help for me in such a big way. I don't know if I could (or would) ever explain to them all that was going on or admit where I was at. They just offered help. With their help the light on the horizon had started to peer in my direction.

I can now look back and see some of what was going on and lessons I needed to learn. It has taken me a good while to find enough humor to start writing again let alone write about some of what was going on with me. It all still seems very raw.

It was not a fun time or situation at all. It is still very hard to think about. I did NOT do well with bits and pieces and all this "divine timing" stuff. It only works if it is on MY timeline. If spirit had just told me the WHY, I would have worked with it. But the words trust and have faith were a massive horse pill to swallow. Have I mentioned I do not do well with pills?

I can honestly say looking back that I feel there were divinely placed friends and a few family members put in my path for support.

There were drop-in messages from spirit, random readings gifted to me without reciprocity and many tangible and intangible gifts. Many were a lifeline for me while I regrouped. I also think that given what was going on in the world people had more (important) things to talk about than my situation if they knew. There was an anonymity element to this as well that I appreciated. It was like they were saying hold on, take a deep breath and breathe!

Someone explained to me a while ago that there are times that you are supposed to just receive. Obviously, I haven't quite grasped this yet. I feel that one of my lessons in the past eleven months was spirit forcing me to receive, trust and have faith. The only way I would listen was for them to strip every conceivable resource away from me, so I had no choice. And that, they did.

I am still working on this. You would think that receiving would be easy. It is not so easy for me. It further explained that the feeling I get from helping someone else is the same one that I needed to let others feel. That I have given and done enough for others and just needed to receive.

They have warned me that there is one more "big thing" coming that I need to hold on to my bootstraps for. Then, the rest will be much smoother sailing. I have been told though that "the hard stuff is over." I can make a mountain out of a molehill at times, so that will remain to be seen.

Looking back, I recall a statement I heard once: If everyone threw their problems in a big pile and you saw what everyone else was dealing with you would go get yours back. I'm sure that is true. I am no exception.

I am also aware of quite a few dreams that I had prior where I had lost my purse, found small pockets of money here and there and my one girlfriend (the ones whose family showed up to help me move) invited me into her house for a few days before I moved. Metaphorically, this situation was that dream.

Regardless, having had the mother of all temper tantrums for eleven months, I know I am still a work in progress. My lessons are not done but spirit did not leave my side.

I don't have all the answers to this time of my life. Like a lot of things, you understand them only when looking back but certainly not while in them.

Things have smoothed out quite a bit since then. When I get to the other side though I am so having a conversation with whoever oversees "divine timing." I have a bone to pick with them and I'm taking my grandpa with me!

3

Toys That Make Noise

I was having a string of frustrating moments trying to fit back in and adjust. Surprised? You shouldn't be! I'm human after all. See, like many of you, I have a very delicate balancing act going on between what I *want* you to see on the outside and what is really going on inside. I am rather good at this charade, too! Don't judge! It's just a lovely coping mechanism I have. Rarely do people ever know what is really going on with me.

Since having moved back to my hometown and there being an ongoing pandemic, I still felt the need to hold myself in high esteem. Yep, looking at me you would never know if there was *ever* anything wrong. I felt I had to act as if I was not affected in any way and had no problems. It was the ole fake-it-till-you-make-it game. Go ahead and roll your eyes and say it with me: sure, you don't. You see, I don't ask for help. I keep a lot of things inside. A great lesson from my mom is that if you don't tell anyone anything, then you can't be judged. Her reward for keeping everything to herself is a collection of ulcers and losing weight. My reward for keeping things in is my neck and ears merge together from stress. Oh, and I eat.

My friend Agent 007 insisted that I come stay in her spare room for a few weeks while in transition. Her husband was on a second shift, so she was going to be alone at night anyway. Walking in the door each evening always started with one of us loudly saying, "Honey, I'm home!"

We had an evening routine and joked like an old married couple. She cooked; I did the dishes. Dinner conversations were always fun because we had someone to talk to about our days.

Boy, did we dish. I forgot how much better it felt to just talk. To trust someone to say what I wanted and how I wanted with no judgment. Everyone should have a friend or two like that. Someone who is safe to blow off steam with, be raw and blunt.

Let me just tell you, I was having a moment and I was very blunt! I was overflowing with unvoiced complaints like a volcano getting ready to erupt. So much angst and internal stress had been building and I had no place to put it. Despite my continued efforts to just be calm, I can attest that I am not entirely efficient in letting everything go just yet. This is a hard side element that I carry on my strong shoulders. Everyone has issues of their own. Do they want mine? Hell, no! Do I take on theirs though? A lot of times I do and don't realize it. I am getting better though!

So, one night after dinner, we carried on with our conversation and a lot just spewed out of me. (I do mean a lot but there was a lot she doesn't know.) She knows about my gifts and spirituality. So, I can talk freely about them.

Adamantly I pulled my soapbox out and complained that so many things were not happening when I felt they should be happening. I was struggling on a few different levels and had yet to speak of them.

Poor Agent 007. What a saint she was listening to me rant. Now, mind you, we took turns vocalizing our strife, but the scales were heavily in my corner this particular evening.

My words were, well, shall I say, not as "PG-13" as they could have been. I let a lot of f-bombs fly. In fact, my motto, and the most common thing I kept saying was this is f-ing stupid! I said it over and over again. I continued to complain and question why things were going the way they were, and how come the timing was not in line with how I felt it should be?

I want to clarify that despite my complaints about what "wasn't," my needs have been more than taken care of. Food, shelter, clothing, and friends. I checked them puppies off the list. It was just so many little nagging things that were irritating me to no end. For about thirty minutes, all I kept saying over and over again was this is f-ing stupid!

Just for the record, Agent 007 and I rarely swear. So, this is way out of character for me. I couldn't help it. I was losing my mind over the details. Guess why? *I was not in control of this season of my life!*

Oh, the bane of my existence, not being in control. UGH!

Anyway, after my rant and spewing more f-bombs than there were blades of grass in the yard, it was time to get our PJs on and watch a scheduled show we were both into. I went into my room and turned the light on.

Agent 007's grandkids use the room I was staying in and it holds their toys and games. There was a toy in the far corner of the room. None of my stuff was anywhere by it, nor did I touch it since being in there. In fact, I didn't even pay attention to it, really.

Until it turned on by itself when I turned on the light at the doorway. I want to clarify that it is battery-operated and not controlled at all by the overhead light.

The centerpiece of it is a smiling face, which is a sign of my great-aunt being around. That is a trademark of hers that I always consider a sign.

The center smiling face lit up yellow.

Then the toy talked: "ENGLISH! ENGLISH!"

(pause)

"ENGLISH! ENGLISH!"

(pause)

"ENGLISH! ENGLISH!"

Let me tell you, it stopped me dead in my tracks at the door. I am pretty sure I said one more f-bomb, but it went along with *what the f@*$* and what did the toy say again?

"ENGLISH! ENGLISH!"

Now, again, I not only had not touched the toy, but I was also about eight feet away from it. It kept saying this! I turned on my

Spidey senses and did not get a bad feeling at all. What did pop into my head was a message from my aunt that said, "*Watch your language, young lady!*" I render that is why the toy was saying (watch your) "ENGLISH!"

Now I had a new level of curiosity. It was simultaneously in slow motion and all at once. I was in the doorway watching this toy turn on across the room from me, and I did that finger move to beckon Agent 007 to come see right-the-freak-now! I never took my eyes off the toy.

I was like, "Agent 007, can you come here please, like *now?*"

We both stood at the doorway and just stared at the smiling face center of this toy lighting up and the voice going, "ENGLISH! ENGLISH!"

She let out a nervous giggle and said, "Well that is interesting!" I told her I hadn't touched it, hadn't even bumped it, and pointed out that none of my stuff was even by it.

So, she moved past me and found the switch and flipped it to (hopefully) turn off. She told me that this particular toy had been up in her attic for twenty-five years, runs on batteries, and that her son played with it when he was little. She questioned if it had a short.

I know that my family, guides, and friends in spirit will play with electronics around me along with an array of many other things to get my attention. I knew that it was their way of communicating with me. They were more or less telling me to quit swearing so much! Talk about getting your hand slapped by spirit! Sheesh!

After a few more moments of quick conversations between Agent 007 and myself, she was about to leave my room when she said, *"There are many more toys in the closet and if they turn on, we are leaving the house!"* I think we both envisioned old scary movies involving evil dolls and toys that have a life of their own. She laughed. I laughed. (The toy laughed … just kidding.) As soon as she left the room, I said out loud to my spirit team, "Nobody better turn on any toys in the closet and freak me out!"

I must admit that little event, lesson, and slap on the wrist did shift my energy. I wasn't angry anymore. Actually, I was a bit more hesitant. Not only did I get off my soapbox, but I kicked it under the bed. The energy that I felt from all that was built up inside of me for a few months was gone. My shoulders dropped a smidgen. I giggled a bit at the craziness of it all. I took a picture of the toy too!

I didn't feel scared at all. I had peace. But under my breath as I fell asleep, I just said, "Please don't let there be a Chucky doll in the closet!"

4

ANGELS WEAR DIAPERS

I have a super strong connection with my granddaughter.

At the time my son and daughter-in-law did not tell anyone that they had considered trying for children. I had a dream one night that my daughter-in-law was in a beautiful, long white nightgown looking out a window. I saw her, looked at her belly, and I asked, "Are you pregnant?"

She said, "Yes! It's a girl!"

I was very excited! Was this prophetic or just something to come? Of course, when I woke up, I wrote this down because I knew and felt in my soul that it was profound. This was one of those dreams that meant something. Although I didn't know the exact time, I still wrote it down.

Two days later, they Face Timed me to announce that they were pregnant! I showed them the piece of paper where I wrote down that

I had dreamt about it. I knew the sex of the baby, but I was not going to tell them.

During the pregnancy, my granddaughter's soul had come through from the other side in many readings, not only to myself but also to others who gave me readings. As the due date came closer, spirit nudged me to do an automatic writing. She wanted to speak to me. I made a note of it on my phone and fell asleep.

I woke up in the morning with this profound feeling that I needed to do it right then. I sat down, did my opening prayers, asked the soul of my granddaughter to step forward and used my hand to write.

Write, she did!

My granddaughter spoke of many things to me. First and foremost, that we share a special bond. There will be many things that she speaks of in wisdom from the other side as she matures and gets older. There will be messages that she will bring forth from the other side to me. I will need to teach her and give her safe space to talk as her mommy and daddy will not fully understand her gifts. She told me that she, too, will also have a daughter who will possess gifts.

Toward the end, she told me that she needed to go. It was time for her to *punch through into this world.*

Less than twelve hours later she was born. She was early.

I was blown away by this! The message was profound—the meaning, and the timing. You can NOT make this stuff up!

Reading it through when I was done, I was in tears. How beautiful and what a *gift*! I have photocopied it and saved the original.

I have read it a few times since and am touched every time. It's just amazing!

Since coming into this world, I have indeed developed a sincere attachment to her. Not only as the first grandchild, or my first granddaughter, but there is a bond of such a soul connection that I cannot explain enough to put into words.

I have gotten in trouble for even holding her too much! The bond is reciprocal as well. Right now, we are buddies and playmates.

One day, spirit sent a beam of sunlight that happened to come through her bedroom window and cross just her eyes and I could see that they were my grandmother's eyes. They were also my eyes.

Since then, I have had the honor of being able to babysit and form a truer connection while she walks this earth. I am down on the floor playing with her, teaching her things, and enjoying the many moments we have. True to her letter to me, I do feel that there is a connection that I have with her.

Spirit has recently given me the message that I will understand her baby babble very soon and I cannot wait. Every morning, when I change her diaper, I ask her if she's got any great stories to tell me from the other side. Spirit also told me that she understands everything that I'm saying to her, which is pretty darn cool. Even though she can't communicate back, I see a level of understanding.

She does a lot for me as well. If I am having a little bit of an off day, she tends to not be as clingy with me to give me my space. Every other day, there is a connection, and we are joined at the hip. There's an energy exchange that we have when she puts her head on my shoulder or when I pick her up. It's a healing energy exchange between us.

If I tried to explain this to somebody else, they would say it was just me being a grandparent and having a granddaughter when I had two sons. It is so much more than that.

I am looking forward to sharing and exchanging wisdom with her. I am excited to offer her a safe space to communicate and share her thoughts, ideas and wisdom from the other side. She's going to be feisty! I want to help foster productivity for the job that she has coming into this world.

I am truly grateful for the automatic writing letter. I'm going to pass it along to her. I have a file for her of things she has done that I feel are magical and fun pictures that aren't posed. I will pass this on to her when she is ready.

My private nickname for her is Houdini. There are some unexplained things that happen when it is just her and me. Most often just a lot of goofy, fun times. She brings out my inner child.

She has a little brother who's going to be born in the next few months as of this writing. There's no doubt that she's got big shoes to fill as the big sister. By far, she has been an insane blessing in my life and has anchored me. The shadow work that I have done to break generational curses in the bloodline will give her a head start in life.

Spirit has also given me the gift of time to foster this relationship with her. The gift is being able to babysit her and create that bond.

I had a dream about her little brother and a different dream that she's going to have a little sister as well! Oh, my son pays very close attention to my dreams at this point! I have a 100 percent hit ratio in the baby department.

She has been such a blessing and a gift to help me in ways that I didn't know I needed to be helped. Something as simple as needing attention, hugs, or just needing to be a kid myself. I have a further excuse to be creative! I build forts. I let her climb. We color, play with sidewalk chalk, and fly paper airplanes. We yell, sing, and dance. So, if nothing else, for two days a week, the little girl inside of ME gets to come out and play with HER. The energy exchange from the hugs and smiles is worth every bit!

She is, indeed, an angel in diapers.

5

CRYSTAL CLEAR

Over the years, I have had different crystals suggested to me during moments when I needed help, strength, or encouragement. I found them to be a talisman to lean on. When the uncertainty in my personal life was intolerable, I leaned on the crystal to make my life more palatable, and to give me strength just as someone might carry rosary beads.

Of course, I would look in every metaphysical store that I was in for whatever stones stood out to me, knowing that there was a reason. I would read the synopsis for the stone, buy it, bring it home and then forget about it in lieu of whatever else was more pressing. As my journey grew more and more profound, I realized that there was indeed some magic behind these stones. Some people will claim they're a bunch of rocks and you can't get power from them. But they are currently used in ultrasound machines, radios, transistors, computer chips, and even digital watches to name a few. They are also used to power amplifiers, electric guitars, microphones, and most digital devices. Sometimes it's just the unknown power that you think something has that gives you the strength to move forward and carry on. As time went on, I found that I was hoarding quite a selection. I found energy in my selected crystals. In fact, I went to a crystal class while in North Carolina, and while they were speaking on the different properties and facets of different stones, there were a few that were passed around for us to individually touch and hold. One absolutely vibrated in my hand that I could not discount, it was so wild. I did not want to put it down for the rest of the class. I even asked the teacher if I could buy it from her to which she said no. The energy from that stone was insane. It had to do with amplifying your psychic skills. It just felt energetically comforting to me, but it also didn't just feel like a stone. It felt like a high vibration of energy.

From then on, I tried to hold and pick up any individual stone that piqued my interest for whatever reason. If I didn't get that same energetic feeling, I would put it down. It was obviously meant for somebody else.

I was sitting in a different crystal class at one point, and someone mentioned how they used crystals to manifest something specific. She further explained that she used a sacred geometry grid and placed specific stones at the intersections to create the energy necessary for manifesting her desire.

Although honestly when I first heard this, I thought *that's fascinating*! that thought was also followed by a "what the hell are you smoking"? Finally, I thought she might be onto something.

I continued to accrue multiple crystals for the different aspects that I needed. Black obsidian was for protection. Amethyst was for opening my heart chakra to allow love back in. Carnelian gave me energy, courage, endurance, and motivation. The list goes on and on. But of course, after I found I had used the different stones for different aspects now, I put them all in a certain place soon to be forgotten for the next latest and greatest polished stone. After a while I couldn't remember exactly what they were or how they were used. I ended up creating my own little laminated flip chart with an actual picture of my stone on it to reference when necessary. While one might go to their jewelry box to pick out the adornment of earrings, necklaces, and bracelets they wanted to wear with an outfit, I looked at my flip chart of my different stones to see what I might need for the day, then promptly put them into my bra.

Well, let me tell you the over-shoulder boulder holder was getting heavy and slightly uncomfortable as the nodules sometimes could be seen through the clothing, which led to a lot of very raised eyebrows!

I had to remember to clear the energy of the stones when I brought them home and put them under the gaze of a full moon for recharging. I feel that they are a great source of extra encouragement, kind of like keeping your lucky penny in your pocket, or worry stone, that you might hold on to for extra strength.

There is no doubt energy behind the stones. Some might argue that it is what you make it, and I agree.

The stones also have created such an energy and a buzz that they belong to me in a way that would not resonate with somebody else. I always encourage someone to acquire a specific stone if spirit recommends it. Your job is to find one that resonates with you the best. Simply accepting somebody else's stone will transfer their energy and should always be cleaned prior to using by waving the smoke of sage or palo santo over it for your own benefit as I feel that energy is transferred.

It's also been a wonderful sort of communication among the rest of the spiritual people in my world. In passing if you see somebody with a tiger's eye bracelet on or certain stones around their neck, you know that they understand something that most other people might not. It's kind of like a super-secret code or handshake.

I adore the crystals that I have and carry a selection of them in my purse. Some I keep on my work desk. I have known other people to keep them in their car.

I have taken a strong interest of late in sacred geometry. It has piqued my interest more often than not. Some days I just don't have enough brain cells to dig in and understand it. I thank the one girl many years ago who spoke of coordinating the stones in a certain shape to create a certain combination of energy. There is a reason that it was put in my path to hear about. Learning more about it is absolutely on my list!

Dear Reader,

If you need encouragement, strength, or protection, I suggest you also research what stones you might benefit from. Do your homework. There are many that align with your chakras as well as what you need help working on. Sometimes, just having it in your pocket is also a source of energy and providing resilience, and a little extra oomph of encouragement that you could need for the day. They're just one extra source to lean on.

6

SPIRIT SAID A BAD WORD

I* am officially tattling on spirit. They said a bad word *through* me in a reading for someone else. Now mind you there have most certainly been some very interesting choice words that they use at times. There are some words I say in readings but don't even know the definition of, let alone how to spell them!

It's funny! I will say the word and sometimes the words right after are "*Here's one of those big words you like.*" It's like they are cupping their wing over my ear and saying that just for me! It is spirit's way of adding humor to keep me out of my left brain. (For those who don't know, the "left brain" is your analytical side.) No doubt, I would immediately start thinking, "*What the hell does that even mean?*" if they didn't say that.

I would like to think I am well-spoken. I love books and reading. There is no doubt I have seen, read, or heard a word I speak but don't always know the meaning, how to spell it, or if I even used it correctly in a sentence!

So, given all of that, it is kind of nice that *I* get a chance to channel my inner five-year-old and tattle on spirit! Yup! (Spoken in my best childlike voice) *Spirit said a bad word!* I don't really know who I am telling this information to exactly. If you're a child, you tattle and tell an adult. But when you're an adult tattling on "the BIG guys/gals/angels," who exactly do you tattle to? Who is above them?

I have been trained to say it like I get it when I am giving a reading. The way in which I say something is meant for the recipient, not for me. I am not to "filter" or "soften" the words. The reason someone's guided to me for a reading is *for* my language. What I say is as important as how I say what I say. It's meant for you to hear it like I would say it, so you absorb it. That being the case I know what is said is for effect. What an effect it had!

Taking that into consideration, I know in normal conversations, inadvertently I may come across as being overly blunt. Just for the record, if *I* think I am being too blunt—it most certainly is super blunt! I have learned that not everyone I read wants it like that.

Another one of my gifts is being empathic; therefore, I sense energy and intention when I am around people. If for some reason I need to, I will ask what version of the message they want to hear. Believe it or not, some people just don't desire to hear anything negative, no matter how spirit spins it. They only want the warm and fuzzy version. I get that and truly respect that as well. I do suspect that if you are reading this, most likely you can handle the humorous suspense of what spirit is going to say and how they say it. Your guess is as good as mine! Laughter does the body good!

I try and remember to tell people I am just the voice for spirit. I receive messages filtered through my own experiences. There is a reason that people are drawn to specific readers as we all possess a unique and individual "filter." Of course, that will be imperative for the delivery and receiving of said message.

I must brag though; my spirit guides have a *wicked* sense of humor! Oh, my goodness! It's so funny when they tattle on the person in front of me. You *know* they hit a nerve when you see shock and awe on the sitters' faces. I love that I get to hear the behind-the-scenes stories as well. Just for the record, I have been the one tattled on before *many-a-time*, so I get it! Trust me! They have tact though. They don't say anything that the sitter can't handle (at least in my experience).

So let me tell you about a reading I did for a friend in my woo-woo group. She and I exchange readings every so often. This group of woo-woo friends are a makeup of like-minded spiritual friends that are also practicing readers. We all have our own skill set of gifts. I assembled us as a group when we needed to practice and get feedback beyond the classes we were taking. We often call on each other to "tap in" to each other's family and spirit guides when we are stuck, need direction, or an answer. It was my turn to help her out.

Yeah, yeah, yeah, I know you're asking why do you need to ask for help when you can do it yourself? Great question! Ever been so close and involved you can't seem to figure out the answer and yet it is right in front of you? Kind of like calling your friend to help them find your phone that is missing when it is the very thing glued to your ear to ask the question. It's like that. Also, to illustrate this, if you have a choice of green or blue and you are leaning toward green, and then ask your spirit guides and get green as the answer, was it really *them* or was it your energy influencing the answer? See? These are things we ask all the time, so we utilize each other. (On a much bigger scale of course.) So, "tapping in" is like our *Google* of the spirit world. Spirits are always on standby and around, so we ask!

Now mind you, you don't always get what you want but *you will always get what you need!* I would also like to stress that they will NOT answer silly questions. Trust me, I try all the time! Yes, they are there to ask but they cannot live your life for you. It is important to trust yourself. Does it stop me from asking? NOPE!

So, my dear friend was having a rough moment and not getting a good feeling about an employer she was interviewing with. She asked me if I could channel and tap in for some answers and guidance on her behalf. Of course, I said no problem! I did my thing and tapped in. She asked the questions and I listened for the answers and reported what they were telling me.

I got a physical description of the gentleman who was to be her boss, should she accept the position. One of the words they said right off the bat to give to her was "MESSATOPIA."

She absolutely busted up laughing at that. She then told me that he was, indeed, extremely messy. Not only his car but also his office! The word "MESSATOPIA" was most certainly all-encompassing although we had never heard it before. Considering that UTOPIA would be something great, a "MESSATOPIA" sounded like a grand scale of a freaking mess! We couldn't stop laughing. You can't make this stuff up!

When we finally stopped laughing, I went on asking for further advice and answers about the subject for her. Spirit gave me the word "*bullsh***" to answer a specific question.

Let me tell you, that was most certainly channeled! Have you ever just had a word or phrase fly out of your mouth so fast you can't retract it? Almost like someone else was saying it. *That's* what it is like and *that's* what happened. I am just the microphone. It wasn't me that said it, it was spirit! Seriously, it flew right out of my mouth. Well, that was just so *overly* appropriate for what the question was, and said so swiftly, we were now wiping tears from our eyes from laughing so hard. We couldn't stop pointing out that *spirit said a bad word*!

In the grand scheme of things, she got what she needed to hear to answer her questions. It was said in such a lighthearted way, again through the filter of my experiences, exactly as she needed to hear it.

Spirit is funny as all get-up! If family or loved ones had a fun personality while they were on earth, they took it with them to the spirit world. If they were stubborn, rough, or unruly, well, they can come across just like that when passing messages on to further give evidence that it's really them!

All in all, spirit took a stressful situation she was trying to wade through and simplified it. Was any of it life and death? Nah. Spirit uses us in ways to help, sometimes through our compassion and understanding and other times through our humor. Personally, I like the humorous version! I always say what I am instructed to using my gifts. It makes it fun when the enhancement of some words gives the truer version of what needs to be said versus the sugarcoated version. Better yet, spirit uses my sense of humor to pass along what is needed to lighten the mood. The mood not only lifted for the sitter (the one getting the reading) but for me as well. Score another one for spirit!

Dear Reader,

Before you sit down with someone to give you a reading, think about and convey to them how you might like to hear the message you are to receive. If you need it raw and blunt, say so. If you need the softer version, say so. Spirit listens and so do we!

7

ME VS. SPIRIT

Hello, my name is Ms. Big Britches. I am the person who has become spiritual in nature but wants permission to wear it like a hat. When I feel like it, I want to take it off and not wear it.

Wait, what do you mean it doesn't work like that?

Despite all the good, oh, there are battles and complaints that I still have. Why can't spirit just do things *my* way?

I have learned that when I go to battle with spirit, despite my efforts, I lose. (Imagine THAT?) The official scoreboard currently reads Lisa: Five, SPIRIT: Ninety-five. Do I stop trying to plead my case in the complaints department? Nope!

My first bone of contention is time. My motto is *schedule-your-work-and-work-your-schedule*. That should include all things spiritual, right? Wrong.

You see, when I am gifted with insightful information, I would like to immediately put it in the puzzle of my life as I see fit and move on to the next project. Does it fit? No. OK, let me rephrase that: *It rarely fits.*

No working ahead, they say. I am to take the information given and sit with it. It appears it could fit the situation *right now* and yet it doesn't. I am left scratching my head yet again. *Excuse me, spirit, why?*

I have spent endless hours going over configurations of who, what, when, and how to no avail.

I picture my angels at times sitting on the other side of the veil saying, "*Watch this one,*" as they toss a ping-pong ball of information to me. Oh, the amusement they must enjoy while watching me scramble to make it fit as I exhaust myself.

So not funny, spirit!

What I have figured out is that they wait for me to get to that point where I give up and then they say, "OK! NOW we will let you see how it fits." Why are some things so slow?

TO: Complaints Department.

SUBJECT: Father Time needs a refresher course in (my) time management.

It's all massively humbling. I feel like I have whispered to my grandfather who is an angel on the other side, "Grandpa, did you talk to the other angels and remind them how important timing is here on earth?" I feel the messages from him back would be in the order of, "*Life goes on and the timelines of others need not apply to your life. You'll get over it. Sorry life misleads you otherwise. I didn't know either.*"

I don't like that I misunderstood timing issues. I seriously have no control over them. Many things have a deadline. Life's calendar and the divine's calendar are not the same. Yet, without ever asking, I got what I needed in the moment they felt was right for me. Was it on "time"? Yes and no.

TO: Complaints Department

SUBJECT: Please be clearer about the messages

Another bone of contention is my interpretation of the messages I am given versus what spirit means. Damn vague statements! We all have seen those sentence examples. Say it one way and it means something completely different than what the speaker was trying to say.

For example, let me use the sentence: "We saw her duck." Off the bat, you can spin this meaning many ways. Where you are at the time dictates how you interpret the message. Is it always the first-case scenario? Nope! I received messages and was plumb proud of myself for figuring it all out at that exact moment, only to realize after a few days that it meant something completely different. Spirit's language is often vague. Dare I even say it can be interpreted as double-talk?

Messages for others are always given with the necessary components. You know it's for you, but goodness gracious, it's amazing how many ways a statement can be taken! I have taken a back seat to interpreting many a statement after an exhausting number of failed attempts and beating my head against the wall. I have concluded that I need to not look at everything at face value until I have more information. Why? Because I am usually wrong at first glance. Life is rarely black and white.

When I get into my super-sleuthing state of mind, watch out. I have figured out all potential storylines, backgrounds and future projected outcomes in every conceivable way. Sadly still, I am rarely *exactly* right. I'm in the ballpark but it's never laid out exactly how *I* think it should have happened. I cannot catch a break to know it all firsthand in perfect timing!

It's a sad game I play alone. They give me a tire and a steering wheel, and I'm convinced I am building a car. I am ready to receive the rest of the parts, I have it painted and a customized license plate ready to go, only to find out that the tire was for a swing in the backyard and the steering wheel was anchored above the tire swing to hold on to. It was not a car at all. GRRR!

This is all maddening to me. No doubt some divine lesson. Of course, once in a blue moon, just when I am ready to give up, I'm right! Yes, you heard me! I am R-I-G-H-T.

It has taken me more years than I will admit getting here. Yes, I have been called stubborn! Old habits are hard to break. (Oh, and I still every so often give it the "ole college try.")

I think what is still frustrating is that I like to work ahead. It has worked in the past! Now every time I try, it feels like I am in that hurry-up-and-wait mentality. Why? Other things have not fallen into place for me to go forward. It could be situations that have not yet arisen or people who have not caught up with me just yet. Dare I also say (*dun, dun, DUUUUNNNN*) unknown parts of the story have not been brought to my attention yet. Working ahead would be futile.

Talk about a learning curve!

I'm sure that there is a Confucius-type statement that applies to this. If you know what it is, let me know! It's all about "when" it is supposed to happen. I have been through the wringer some days, with frustrations over what is to happen and when.

My inner child has thrown many a temper tantrum over these moments. I know I asked for the receiving of these messages from spirit. I still question why tell me if I can't do anything about it? Their answer?

Faith.

Patience.

Understanding.

I do sometimes try reverse psychology with spirit thinking I am beating the system. They have no problem reminding me that they know my every thought and are onto me. Oh, I feel my spirit team is clapping and slapping high fives to each other. Therefore, my spirit team's score is ninety-five and mine is not!

It's *maddening* I tell you!

It is a constant mental battle for me. I question if I did my part, and did enough? More often than not, it is more peaceful to just surrender. I know that I am protected. I know that in my heart of hearts I am a good person. I have seen many blessings materialize in ways I never thought would happen or could comprehend because I just let things be. Most I never saw coming. What is meant for me will never pass me by.

It makes sense that my complaints fall on deaf ears. Spirit is winning hands down!

8

Drop-in Messages from the Rocker

Sometimes I feel like I've been broken twice. The first time was an unspoken battle of wills with my now ex-husband. That one-year marriage did a number on me. Mind you, this was all behavior I allowed. Somewhere deep down I felt I deserved it or did not know my own worth. Note taken. I tracked this learned behavior all the way into my childhood. That is what shadow work does. It makes you dig deep into the origins of it all. Found it! Fixed it and filed it away for future reference if needed.

Although it felt like my spirits were lifting again, a lot of times it felt like I was constantly taking two steps back for every step forward. It was in the form of strife, lack, and indecision that I went through with no explanation. At every turn for a while, it felt like another proverbial shoe dropped in my life. Anything that I felt was good would vanish. It taught me to hold on to nothing.

The lack of stability that seemed like a constant battering in my life for a while is what I felt broke me twice. I have always taken great pride in being able to take care of myself. This was a time that I wasn't 100 percent back on my feet just yet. That is what broke me the second time. It was starting to feel like a military boot camp when they break your spirit down to rebuild you back up. Think you are strong? Down and give me twenty!

I say all that with love and respect. I just didn't understand why when I was doing everything right that I had to endure what I did.

Gratefully, I absolutely had a roof over my head, the bare necessities, and the health of myself and everyone around me. I am 1,000,000 percent sure that I have been protected in ways that I will never understand by my spiritual guardians and guides.

During one of my times of despair when there seemed to be yet another setback, spirit gave me the knowledge of future events coming forth for me in a vision. The event held tremendous promise but there was no official date or time so there was nothing solid to hang my hat on just yet. It was just a heads-up.

So, one afternoon when things had settled down again, I was rocking my granddaughter to sleep. Suddenly I received a message from spirit again to go along with what they had already informed me of. The message was: *Pay attention to who has helped you in the recent times of strife when you had nothing to give in repayment. Remember who was there for you. But more importantly who was not. Take note of this.*

OK, that was interesting! I did indeed take a few minutes and recalled all of those that helped me and *those that didn't.*

Spirit then further explained: *It was necessary for you to have had this recent experience because it helped you truly understand things you need for your future. You will understand this in times to come.*

Of course, I'm thinking I'm going to have a story to tell. Obviously, I do because you're reading it.

Learning what I have thus far, the people that reached out to help me are indeed my truest friends. They've now seen me broken twice and didn't run away.

It was good to take note so whatever happens in the future, I will remember in case they are looking for a handout.

Notwithstanding, I must call a spade a spade. I'm extremely private. I don't tell anybody about my business except for a select few. Would anyone else have offered help without judgment if I was forthcoming about things? Honestly, I don't think some would have. Sad, I know. I will remember those that paid attention and did help.

I realize that in the big picture, I have done many things for many people, never expecting, or receiving anything in return. That is how and who I am. My friends and some family did the same for me. The entire time was a huge lesson for me in many ways.

Dear Reader,

I am just like you and don't always understand at the time why things happen. I encourage you when you can to step back and look at things from the bigger picture. What is it that you are supposed to know or learn? Looking at it this way does help to take the edge off. If you don't know, ask. You might be surprised by what you are told.

9

ENERGETIC RESIDUE

I recently looked up and learned what energetic residue is. It is energy left where emotionally charged events have taken place. I didn't know this was possible, but it makes perfect sense! Here is the Wikipedia description: *Locations where much physical life was lost, and great suffering has occurred, may leave a particularly long and strong negative energetic imprint. Such negative residual energy is not always easily cleared and may be experienced many years later.*

Wow!

What instantly came to mind when I was reading this was an incident while visiting Saint Augustine, Florida, with some friend's years ago. One of the things on our list was to visit the local prison. It is an old Spanish fort that has a lot of history!

Seemed innocent enough. I did remember asking spirit to put some protection around me while we were waiting in line. It was just a feeling I had for some unknown reason.

We all shuffled into the jail listening to the tour guide tell the history and relay stories about the prison. Looking around, there were some jail cells I just felt I could not go into as some people were. Hell, some were lying on the beds and congregating. Not me! There wasn't a specific reason, it was just a feeling. Just a strong nudge to NOT go in but look from afar. Looking from the outside-in was enough. In one cell there was a window out to the back of the jail, and I could clearly see a noose used for the criminals at that time. Dang!

We all stood in the center area between the two rows of jail cells, listening to the information the guide was giving, and I suddenly couldn't breathe and started coughing. So much so that I was escorted out. Once outside, I took quite a few deep breaths and got something to drink. I felt energetically that I was not to go back in there at all. I didn't.

That situation popped up when I read the description of energetic residue and *now* it made perfect sense!

Another not-so-dire example of energetic residue applies to women who feel the need to cut their hair after a breakup or divorce. I have done this in the past. I never knew exactly what for other than I wanted a change, so I just did.

After many discussions with fellow girlfriends, I think we surmised it was the "clean slate, glow up" thing. It goes along with putting more time and effort into yourself where the side effect was you just felt better! Oh, there are even standing jokes about it on social media for sure! "Ladies, leave your hair alone!" Whether it was a placebo effect or not, I don't know. Cutting *the hair* just seemed to put an oomph in my step.

Coincidentally, I came across someone explaining how the desire is *because* of energetic residue. Yes, the hair that grew during the good times and the bad in your relationship was still attached to you. I never thought of it that way!

The energy we carry and store in our bodies is an accumulation of good and bad experiences, instances, and traumas. Just like a location can hold on to "energy" from times past, so does our cellular structure.

It is a stark reminder that energetic residue is not only in our hair but everywhere. The words and situation all carry energy and are not always good.

This explains why you can walk into a room where people have been fighting and just *feel* the wonky energy. Energy is everywhere!

I am sure, knowing what I know now, that there have been many other instances where I just didn't attribute the energy or shift in what I felt to energetic residue. Cutting off the energetic ties—or your hair—does help to give you a fresh start though!

Chop! Chop!

Dear Reader,

I would suggest looking up the chakra system and learning about it. When you learn about these energy places in your body, you might see how some ailments are stored in your system. It is rather fascinating once you know!

10

LIFE SCHOOL

It goes without saying that I have a very vivid imagination. Call it a protection mode but it also helps when trying to describe things that come to me to make sure others understand. I use this for myself to often take the edge off messages and explain them to others. It's my way of taking the energy out of a situation and lightening the mood as well. Again, not only for others but for myself!

When my woo-woo group and I exchange readings, they often get cartoonish and comedic visuals to give to me. They too don't overthink what they are to give to me. We all often laugh about it! Spirit knows I can't overanalyze the messages if they are described to me by Snoopy and Woodstock among others, doing fun and goofy things.

Delores Cannon spoke of many things spiritual over the years before she passed. She has explained that earth is a "school." I cannot agree more.

In the many lessons that I have learned over the years along with the temper tantrums I have had, I have described the "spiritual side" as a sort of school, in my own way. It has been a standing joke of mine to say, "When I get back to the spiritual realm, I'm going to …"

Spirit keeps telling me that I have a unique way of looking at things, so this is how I feel it looks on the other side.

Here it goes: **MY EXPLANATION AND VISUAL OF THE OTHER SIDE, BEFORE WE GET TO EARTH.**

THE OFFICIAL SOUL GROUP MEETING

There are soul groups. These are the people we come back to earth to work with. All the spirits gather in their assigned group and meet up in some big auditorium. Together they decided among themselves what part they want to play in life this time. One soul might speak up and say *I want to be the mom!* Another might say *I want to be a bad person!* Mind you, there are some that continue to play the same part over and over again—albeit perfecting it even more. Once every soul decides on what part they are going to play, they are led to the lunch line. In the lunch line, they pick the "experiences" they want to have. Think of it like a school lunch line à la carte.

THE LUNCH LINE OF EXPERIENCE

It has been said that every experience we have in our life is something that we choose to have. Just bear with me while I put on my rose-colored glasses to say this. Frankly, all the good things—yes.

We choose the good. The bad stuff? The *awful* things? Well, I can't fathom that someone actively chooses to participate in those. I am told that we do, though. Frankly, I don't understand it but that's my lesson to learn.

I picture all the souls getting their trays and going through the lunch line, announcing to the lady behind the counter with a hairnet and white smock what experiences they are choosing to have in their life. So, one soul might ask for the "marriage" experience. Then the "options" are I'll have a side of cheating and divorce and all variations of that life. Another soul might ask for the "career" package, with the optional packages of material gain and loss. Some souls might ask for the "mystery and dread package," with the options of not fitting in and abandonment. Another might ask for the road less traveled experience, with a side of small experiences and inspirational people, places, and events.

Every soul in this group must pick what "experience" package they want for the life they are coming into. There are many to choose from and only so many of each. Not everyone can be president!

Everyone in line must take at least one wild card experience. I liken this to be the "mystery meal/meat in a lunch line." You're not sure what you're going to get but once it "goes off"—you are awakened and must do the work to get back to "home base." Kind of like having a clock with a predetermined time and date. Once it goes off (triggering an awakening experience), then you must dig yourself out to learn the lesson before you get back home—or better put— BACK TO THE FUTURE!

HELP DEPARTMENT

While the souls all sit around discussing what experiences they picked, there is the help department. These are the "chaperones" of the soul group. They all have roles to play as well. They are the souls and angels that decide to stay in the background and assist this time. In other words, the support system.

I picture them like the set directors, costume makers, makeup crew, musical scoring, advertisement, planning, secretaries, and directors of this group's path. They are the ones that mess your life up until you go down a different path. They are the ones that hold things up for your own good—even though you're frustrated and don't see why. These are the souls that make you drop things to slow you down to pay attention. These are the souls that make sure you see what you need to see, know what you need to know, and feel what you need to feel to successfully learn the lesson of that experience.

Standard accessories, through my eyes, are like a magic wand they flick to do all of this. I can't tell you how many times I have a visual of an angel sitting on my shoulder, legs crossed, filing her fingernails, chewing gum, saying, "not happening"! Or whispering in my ear—*you really should listen to this part*!

ASSISTANTS TO THE HELP DEPARTMENT

The assistants are runners and helpers; you know the ones. They help find your keys or shoes when you are running late, help you find the perfect parking spot you ask for and put synchronicities in front of you when you need them. So, while the general "operations" of the experiences are in full force and everyone is moving different things into our paths and making sure the right people show up at the right part, these assistants make sure the details are handled or observed.

AVATAR/FLESH-SUIT DEPARTMENT

Before the start of production, your soul needs something to wear. They all head over to the costume department. Oh, I want to go back and repick out my "avatar" some days.

We are all souls inside a body. This flesh-suit we wear, well, it's on rent for now. We are in charge of keeping it clean inside and out. (As I slowly push the candy corn away from the computer while I'm typing this.)

Sometimes it comes with defects and imperfections that are a result of choices we make. It is ours to keep and will expire when we leave life school. New avatars are constantly regenerated for new and upcoming soul groups. No two are exactly alike. When we are born, we receive a new avatar that will grow and stretch with us and, when we are done here, we leave it and float, unencumbered, back "home."

After we have picked out the avatar and have our lunch line of experiences, we are ready to check out and get started. Are you really ready though? Is it that easy? Nope! You also have to pass through and pick up your "mystery" packet of homework.

THE KARMA DEPARTMENT

This is like the study hall or time-out office. All the main souls get a report from the assistants to the help department. Yup, they tattle on us too! Those "rebels" who aren't getting the "lessons" that they took on to learn. I envision a large conference table and one strong light beaming down in the center. There is a pile of files of those souls that keep doing the same thing over and over again and not getting the lesson to move on. The karma department is there to make sure that they are not consistently rewarded. I picture a holographic visual of their situation and circumstances like a movie in the middle of the table.

This department meets to discuss how long they are going to give that soul to straighten up and get back on track before they step in with "divine timing" and make them wake up and pay attention (e.g., traumatic life event). Kind of like the wake-up clock they brought with them has been jammed up and ignored. They all review a copy of what the soul chose for this life and put in place a strict timetable for them going forward. They have the assistants to the helpers give "warning shots." If there is still no formal action, they agree upon the big stuff to happen to them, they write it up and hand it off to the helpers' group and put them on notice. I am pretty sure at the top of this report it is titled "SH*T's ABOUT TO GET REAL FOR THIS SOUL." A duplicate copy then gets sent to Father Time.

FATHER TIME

Oh, so much to say about Father Time and that dang hourglass he carries. First of all, it needs recalibration. *Tick tock, tick tock.* I would also like to start a GoFundMe page for Father Time to get new glasses, and a new hourglass. Father Time's time and MY time are not the same. I see perfect opportunities for things to happen and yet they don't. So what exactly is divine timing anyway. I see it like a golden grain of sand that, when it finally makes its way through the neck of the hourglass, opens up the neck wider for more to happen. That is when "divine timing" happens.

RETURNS DEPARTMENT

Finally, there is the returns department. When our time is up here at earth school and we have completed what we were supposed to, our body ceases to exist in one way or another based on what programs we chose. Our ticket is mysteriously up, and we are released from our life here on earth and excused to go home. Not all returns are happy ones and not all are sad. It just depends.

REVIEW AND GRADING DEPARTMENT

Upon being released from our avatar, we go to the "review department." I picture a big white interrogation room with a single chair and a strong beaming light. I also imagine Morgan Freeman's voice over a loudspeaker, going over our chosen assignments and tasks we were supposed to accomplish. We get a flash movie of it all so there is a visual. We then get graded on what we did and didn't do compared to our original choices. Once we have finished with this department, we are excused and free to go back to the waiting pool of souls and start the process all over again.

NEXT GRADE OR REPEATING A COURSE

Those who passed get to go back to another soul group meeting to pick out the next part they want to play. There is always a group of souls that didn't accomplish what they set out to do or learn the lesson they were meant to learn. Guess what? They have to come back and do it all over again.

The end.

So, that is what I think it looks like on the other side before we get here. I think that as we are traveling through the portal and being born, our brains and thoughts are reset until that activation clock goes off. That's why we all look so cute and innocent in the beginning.

I have many questions for these departments when I cross back over. The first stop on my list will be the karma department. I see myself bursting past Archangel Michael at the door and interrupting the big conference of all the other big angels, demanding to know *who's in charge of that department and why so-and-so hasn't gotten their karma! Also why do they look like they are rewarded over and over again with happiness and great experiences?* (If you want me to ask about your situation and circumstances, please fill out the attached forms and I will also ask for you! Just kidding.)

After that, I'm taking Father Time out for coffee. He is in need of a *very* long talk. I picture him like Dumbledore from the *Harry Potter* movies. I plan on volunteering for the "experiences" committee as well. I fail to understand the concept of how someone could choose some *really tough experiences,* and others are just having a cakewalk rose-colored glasses experience. Why can't we all have a field trip with rainbows, unicorns, and butterflies?

As you can tell, I have thought long and hard about all of this. I am still just a soul in my avatar, having lessons at my earth school. I don't know who to file a complaint with or give a compliment to about all of this. I have yet to find where there is a YELP or Google review platform for life school. It's been a wild ride and, honestly, compared to some experience's others have had, I am really and truly grateful. I know I have said it before and I will say it again—if everyone in your soul group threw all their experiences into a pile for you to see, you would most likely go grab yours back.

Alas, my "wild card" experience went off and I have had a spiritual awakening. I have proceeded with great caution yet learned many lessons. They were mine to learn. They don't make sense to anyone else—no matter how I would explain it. All I can hope is that I get a good grade for all that I have done this time. I am really over this learning lesson stuff. It would be nice if it were just recess!

11

POP QUIZ: FAIL!

Spirit decided it would be a great time over *Christmas* to see how I would handle an unforeseen situation. I completely messed it up. Let me explain.

One of the great gifts that I received from spirit this Christmas was not only being back in town with both my kids but also the opportunity to have resources to give gifts. It was a rough year financially with moving and getting reestablished. Having a few dollars to buy presents this year was a biggie for me.

Was not being able to give a Christmas present really a hardship for me to bear? Yes! Why? I'm a giver. Not being able to give was embarrassing and a massive slam to my heart.

I have had so much help and gifts given to me by various people over the past year. The need to give back was very near and dear to my heart. I truly wanted to, no, *needed* to do something really super special for Agent 007 and her husband, for the generosity that they have bestowed upon me. Nothing they did for me was a loan, came with unspoken expectations, or had any deadlines or obligations attached to their help, at all. In my prayers, I asked spirit to really give them something that I could not. Something that would

stand above and beyond and there would be no question where it came from.

I told Agent 007 of my request from spirit for her. She let me know that they both indeed had received a few things way above and beyond what she was ever expecting. She feels that was the gift! She wasn't expecting anything but the last time I put a request in for something to be done for her in gratitude, she and her husband both got some hellacious raises and bonuses to boot! I didn't know how or what would manifest. I just believed something would. I believe it was spirit's way of saying THANK YOU to them through the hands of others. That was part one. I was able to give, and spirit did too!

The second part of my Christmas was amazing as well! My oldest son and his wife announced in a very creative way that they were going to have *their first child*. Being very creative myself, their efforts touched my heart. Spirit did not tattle and spill the secret beforehand either! They let them tell me in their own way! Oh, happy day! I'm going to be a Mimi again! My heart was even fuller!

By now, you're probably thinking—jeez, it sounds like a great Christmas! How could I flunk a pop quiz?

Oh, sadly, I did.

Let me just explain the short version.

While with my oldest in North Florida, there was some sort of a texting feud going on between my two kids and their wives. Again, on Christmas Day. I had no idea what it was about. I only heard bits and pieces. I heard words like "they told." Told what? I had no clue but given how frustrated they were I assumed that what "they told" was spilling their secret of being first-time parents to whomever they were with. *Did I ask?* Nope! I want to stress that they didn't offer me any information either. Did my intuition kick in and tell me something more was going on? Probably. Did I listen though? Nope! I rendered my intuitive self "off" for the day. I didn't shift my energy to do any psychic or intuitive work. (My bad!)

My goal was to do like my amazing former mother-in-law did and stay out of drama between siblings and their spouses. I just was not going to get involved.

I was plum proud of myself for this. I didn't ask any questions. I didn't read any text messages. (Nor were any offered for me to see.) All I heard was that one of my daughters-in-law spilled the beans. I assumed that she spilled the beans about the oldest having a baby before they were able to. (Remember, I didn't know the full picture.) Looking back, I want to stress that not knowing the entire story nor asking about what was going on wasn't the best choice on my part.

It was time for me to drive four and a half hours home and stop at my youngest and his wife's home to celebrate Christmas with them. I was on guard going in. I didn't want to get dragged into a he-said/she-said disagreement. I didn't know anything, and I wanted to keep it like that.

So, there were happy exchanges and small talk and snuggles from my granddaughter. I could feel the unspoken tension. I did what I thought was best and avoided the elephant in the room.

Leading comments were made here and there, and I knew they were trying to bring up the subject. They wanted my perspective and to tell their side. I didn't want to have anything to do with it and politely told them so. I point-blank told them that whatever it is, I am staying out of it. So, I did what I have always unconsciously done and changed the subject. My guard was up.

So, when my daughter-in-law had made a comment that my granddaughter was going to be a big sister, I did not hear the true context. With my guard up, all that flew through my head was *of course* she was! She was going to be a big sister-ish person to my oldest son's and his wife's new baby! On top of that, my daughter-in-law's sister was also due to have a baby. Being the oldest, my granddaughter would take on being more like a big sister!

Seriously, I should have tattooed the word *ditz* on my forehead. *I was listening to defend, not to understand.*

Again, I want to stress I was on guard and trying to act like I wasn't. Another *bad move*. This is another bad habit of mine that I need to change. You know, if I were an ostrich, you could envision me with my head in the sand. I thought I was doing the right thing. I so wasn't.

So, is this why I failed my pop quiz? HA! Yes! But for extra credit, there's more that I flunked!

Rightfully so, my daughter-in-law was pretty offended by me being so dismissive of *their* news.

Their news still had not registered with me. I never put two and two together. My son and daughter-in-law even had my granddaughter wearing a cute little shirt that said SISTER.

Super frustrated, my daughter-in-law called me an un-nice word, got up, and stormed out of the room for not listening to their side. My poor son sat there in shock, not sure what to do. At this point I didn't know what to do either. What was happening? My granddaughter was going to be a big sister to her cousins, and I didn't want to get involved in their feud.

Christmas was going swimmingly well as you can tell.

I hugged my son and he whispered to me that he didn't want to lose his brother over this but would stick up for his family. I understood this but I didn't have an answer. I said goodbye and left.

Driving away I kept feeling that I did not have the full picture. *What the hell was going on?*

I went to Agent 007's house and told her what was going on. I had no clue what had happened. I didn't want to get into the middle of their fight, and I was called out because I made a choice to not get involved. Like, seriously?

Suddenly my phone rang. It's my oldest son very firmly telling me that I needed to help and do damage control!

I finally just said WHAT THE HELL IS GOING ON? (Flamingo finally removes head from sand.) He said, **MOM! THEY**

ARE PREGNANT TOO, AND THEY THINK WE TOLD YOU FIRST!

Wait, **what?** Oh no, no, no, no, no.

They were pregnant too? I cannot express how far-fetched it is that I didn't put two and two together. I-JUST-DIDN'T. In hindsight, I think spirit did this on purpose to force me to learn some lessons about myself. That, I did.

So that rendered me getting back in the car after a nine-hour drive back and forth from North Florida and go back over to my youngest son's house. I banged on their door and announced, *"Family meeting!"*

I went in and explained my side of the story. They did not believe me that I had no idea. I understood their point of view. They thought my oldest son had told me. *He didn't.* It wasn't his announcement to speak! I respected that!

After a bunch of back-and-forth comments, I had tears streaming down my face and very loudly said, *"I did not move back from North Carolina to have my family destroyed. This shit has got to stop!"*

Folks, the pop quiz was over. Grade: FAIL.

I reacted and didn't respond. I lost my cool in defense of myself. Spirit was putting a big red "F" on my pop quiz. I got brownie points for standing up for myself and *speaking my truth.* I did *that* correctly. It was how I handled the rest that was wrong. Even in my former way of being, I rarely, if ever, acted like that. I was exhausted but that was no excuse.

(*Ding ding ding*! Give that woman a prize!)

The line in the sand was drawn now with my son and daughter-in-law.

Spirit probably figured enough damage was done and I channeled my words out loud to them both: "I have never been a mother-in-law before. I have only been the daughter-in-law. I don't know what to do to fix this, but you have my word I did not know, and no one told me."

I reminded them how excited I was when I found out they were having my granddaughter so why would I be dismissive of them having a second child?

We were all upset but things finally calmed down. We all apologized. I said my goodbyes and went home, emotionally spent.

Of course, I was thinking of a million things I did wrong. Jeez, I had done all this inner work, and this is how I acted? What kind of an example am I if I act like this?

In my defense, I did a few things right. I kept reminding myself that the entire fight was not about me. It was between the kids regarding who stole the limelight of their individual announcements. In my opinion, the confusion on their part was that both were making the announcement to their father and me (divorced) in two different areas of the state and making assumptions based on misconstrued text messages. I was caught in the middle because I put my head in the sand thinking I was keeping peace. How wrong I was.

Spirit was, in a way, making me stand up in front of the class and explain what I did right and wrong. I was exhausted from my day driving but it was still my fault because I did not *ask what was wrong.* I assumed and did not have the full picture.

The biggest part was that I reacted and did not respond. Seriously, if you know me, you know that reacting the way I did is way out of character. In times of conflict, I negotiate and keep a very even temper. I don't take things personally. I am a voice of reason and calm as I look at things from both perspectives. This time though? Not even close!

No doubt, spirit gave me this little pop quiz for reflection and study for future pop quizzes. I was very self-aware to figure out my part and what I learned. A big one is that it is OK to be vulnerable and be involved in some situations. Everyone deserved to be heard. I need to have better communication and sticking my head in the sand is not an option, especially with family. The good news is I am going to have two new grandbabies!

Spirit let me know they'll both be boys! I am very excited. I hugged my granddaughter this week even more because she and I will have a special bond that cannot be broken but I am going to adore having two little boys to spoil as well.

So, the POP QUIZ Christmas edition was a FAIL! I will know better next time! Lesson learned!

12

WORDS MEAN A LOT

It took forever but I am finally back out on my own and completely self-sufficient. I've been able to repay monies that were loaned to me. I am not out of the woods yet. I just want to stress that I am overwhelmingly grateful! I am not taking *anything* for granted. It is rather nice to feel calm and settled again.

I'm still sleeping on an air mattress. I don't have a dresser so thank goodness for Piggly Wiggly bags that hold my undergarments that I hang in my closet.

I ordered my storage container of belongings that includes my furniture. It'll be here in about a week's time. I can tell you that living out of a suitcase and basically not having most of your personal stuff with you makes you really analyze what you do and don't need. I've never been materialistic, but I have taken care of what I have bought, so it's lasted.

I thought about all that's inside the container and asked myself what I am most excited about. It is my family photos and videos. It is the autobiographies of my grandparents and some things from them that mean a lot. I am extra excited to have the space and the opportunity to get all my woo-woo stuff out again, including all sorts of oracle cards, journals, channeling, and dream notebooks.

I sat down and channeled for myself again. There's always a menagerie of many different subjects they touch on when they speak to me. One of the things that they suggested is that I should reread all the messages that they have given me thus far starting from the initial channeling books. They asked me to look at their words and I will see all that has come forth that they spoke of. I'm actually kind of excited about that!

In addition to doing that, I have a lot of repeat people who come back to me for readings now. I've struggled with some of the messages that I get because to me they're not necessarily all rainbows, butterflies, and unicorns. I want to be a source of inspiration not the Debbie Downer of bad news. I know spirit is very careful with how they give me the information so that I don't speak it in a way that evokes fear at all, but you truly never know what's going on with somebody.

For example, I recently did a reading and one of the first words out of my mouth was "benign." I remember when I got it, there was a flash of thinking I don't want to say that word because that must have to do with cancer. I honestly did not know what benign meant. Was it the good news or the bad news? I learned long ago to say exactly what I'm getting from spirit when I channel. My job is to deliver messages. It is not to interpret, understand, or explain it. It was not for me.

After the reading was over, we talked for another forty minutes. She mentioned that she's been getting pain in her breast. She didn't know if it was a manifestation of things that she was going through at that time or if it was something more serious. I reminded her that one of the first words that came out of my mouth was *benign*. It wasn't until after we parted ways that I looked the word up. Knock on wood, I don't have a big education in cancer terms or know what that word meant. It was a good word. It was just a reminder to me to absolutely speak what I receive.

Another repeat client called for a reading a few days ago. After the reading she mentioned she was really looking for some inspiration again from the reading. I felt so honored. It wasn't me she was looking for inspiration from but spirit. She explained that the messages that she's received from me in the past have been inspiring and hopeful. That truly touched my heart in a big way. Although no message is ever all rainbows, butterflies, unicorns, and buckets of money, my language and delivery help others. I've heard that from many people, now that I'm thinking about it, and I'm very grateful.

I have been to readers in the past who, with their words, put out just enough "bait." Just enough teaser statements that if taken the wrong way could evoke fears. You know, just enough to get someone to book another reading from them. I won't be that person. I want to inspire, inform, and gift whatever messages are given through me.

Looking back at the readings I had received in the past, I realize now what a gift most messages were when I needed them the most.

During moments of extreme stress, I literally hung on to every word as gospel. A few times though, I got some really bad advice that was NOT the best for me. I realized that the reader's personal life was bleeding into the reading. I can look back and remember I felt it was bad but wrote it off making some very big mistakes because of it. Now on the other side of the fence and giving readings, I read only when my energy is high and ask for uplifting information, so the recipients part ways feeling empowered and strong.

Words are very powerful. You never know how they are going to affect someone. It just reminds me of the chapter in the book *Four Agreements*, "Be Impeccable with Your Words."

Dear Reader,

The words you speak to others affect them in ways you may not always understand. This also applies to the words you speak to yourself. It is a reminder to always be kind and gentle. Everyone has their own unhappy thoughts and ideas to deal with. Don't add to them.

13

LESS IS MORE, MORE OR LESS

Everyone has their own lessons and issues to deal with. On my journey, I have been challenged to address my feelings. This has never been easy for me. I know they are a barometer of what is going on inside and I had always ignored them before. Not ignoring them is new to me. So, I now attempt to honor my feelings. Like many, my emotions had been dismissed growing up. As an adult, I further dismissed or bottled them up. Emotions for me were not allowed, labeled weak, and a waste of time. Crying solved nothing. I have since worked to change this part of me. I am a work in progress. So, guess who started crying when they saw a delivery truck with the pod of their belongings roll up to be delivered? THIS gal.

I wasn't expecting *this* reaction. Jeez, it's just a box with stuff in it! Right? Well, everything was different when it was packed compared to now. There was a realization that I had indeed taken quite a few steps forward in life and all that had been accomplished since.

I just pictured my alter ego standing next to me going *seriously, you're crying over a box. It's a box that has stuff in it.* To me though, it was much more than that. Not only was it my personal belongings but it also represented in some way that I had arrived.

I can honestly say I was very caught off guard by all of this. Seeing that container holding my stuff that had been in storage for ten months meant so much that I don't think I could even put it into words. There was such a sense of gratitude for this seemingly small but monumental accomplishment to get it to Florida from North Carolina.

There is indeed a lot of work ahead to unpack. It will be worth it to get my bed and pillow back!

Spirit hung out with me as I unpacked. I visualized them sitting on the kitchen counter passing messages to me while I felt overwhelmed wondering where to put everything. I kept hearing spirit say, "*We told you to sell everything.*"

Yes, they did. I remember getting that message thinking, *OK that's random!* The bigger question I had, that they did not give further explanation of at the time, was what everything was and WHY. Did they tell me? Nope. So, did I listen? Nope.

I needed them to define "everything." Was it literally one of everything or just housewares? Although, comparatively speaking, I didn't have a lot but when you have nothing for a while, well, all my stuff suddenly *seemed* like a lot!

I was further reminded of another channeled message I received when I was packing up in North Carolina to put my stuff in storage for the move back. It was, *"You only need one good pot and one good pan, and the rest can go."*

UGH.

The message felt cryptic to me at the time because of them not explaining why. Was I going to be camping? Living out of my car? How was I supposed to cook for more than one person with only one good pot and one good pan? Of course, now I understand what they were saying. Unpacking in Florida, I picked out one pot and pan and put the rest in a donation pile.

So, as I further unpacked spirit dropped in another thought: You have lived without all this stuff for almost a year. Do you really still need it?

You know, after that comment I assessed all the boxes that were still yet to be unpacked. Maybe they had a point. Did I really need what was inside? Probably not all of it. Unboxing it was, though, like Christmas!

Spirit then reminded me of my stress levels and how I felt things were simpler without excess. OK, life was simpler at times and inconvenient at others. Note taken.

Needs and wants are a very tricky word exchange. What I consider and you consider a need may be two completely different things.

Being this self-aware is exhausting, I tell you!

As I continued to unbox, the donation pile grew exponentially. Spirit continued to remind me that less is more. I'm truly starting to believe it. With so much left to unbox, I feel swallowed by "stuff." Living without was simple in some ways and difficult in others. It's about perspective.

So, it goes without saying: Less is more, more or less. I still feel there are bits and pieces of gray area in that statement.

The latest message from spirit was the reason for purging and organizing is because of another upcoming move. SOON.

You know, I had a premonition prior, of me pointing out boxes to professional movers to load in a truck from the space that I currently live in. So, this made sense. No more information has been revealed to me just yet. It is obvious there are more changes on the horizon for me. Gifting me the time to make decisions about my stuff was greatly appreciated.

Now that I am seeing more and more how spirit works it would be nice if I had a time frame.

WISH ME LUCK!

Dear Reader,

Take a few moments and really look at all that you have accumulated. So much could be donated or given away that you don't need or use any longer. Reassessment is very eye-opening and helpful. Just a thought!

14

MISSING PERSON EXERCISES

I am sort of the "grand poo-bah" of the practice group I put together while I lived in North Carolina. I want to stress that we have all come such a long way that I hate saying it's "practice" any longer. It is more of a woo-woo exchange group now. We have all settled into our gifts nicely and are not testing the waters much. We have confidence that we didn't have before. We all work with our gifts in our own ways.

I like coordinating themed activities for our gatherings. One evening, it might be spirit art, another psychometry or mediumship. I try to keep it interesting with anything that involves metaphysical practices.

Our core group is now all over the United States, as our lives have pulled us in different directions. Due to COVID and many moving, we are holding our meetings via Zoom now. We enjoy and appreciate that we have a safe place to practice some or all the modalities we have access to.

Last month, as a group, we were presented with a situation of a legit missing person. This was a personal friend of someone in our group.

We all awoke to a group text at 4:30 a.m. pleading for us all to see what we could get and what came to us. She explained to us the call from a family member with some disturbing information.

We were asked to "tap in" and report our findings. The person initiating this request had tapped in but knew that her personal feelings were getting in the way of any clear answer or direction, which they often do.

We have performed this kind of practice before a few times, but it always involved someone who could validate the information for us. This was a *legit* missing person's case. All we could do was report what information spirit gave us and wait to see what happened.

I tapped in and gave the information received from my angels and spirit guides. Others did the same. It is always interesting to see how some of us got extremely similar information and others got another, different, piece or aspect. We do not all get the same information at the same time. Doing this spiritual work, we know and understand it is important that all information be taken with a grain of salt. It is not that we don't get valid information, it is being in the right frame of mind to receive it and interpreting what we receive.

Our friend told us that she reported all the information we gave to the local authorities. She also told us they rolled their eyes at her when she told them where this information came from. She was NOT happy! Frankly, she was angry they were not taking our information seriously as a lead. If that were my friend or family missing and any lead was not taken into consideration, I would be angry too!

She did get back to us later and thanked us for helping. She validated that some of our information about the missing person and their location was, indeed, correct. They found the person. Sadly, they had taken their own life.

Another instance where we used our skills recently was a cold case that someone in our group agreed to look into. She presented us with a picture to tap in and see what we all got. Between our psychic, mediumship, and intuitive abilities, again, those who wanted to participate did and reported what they received. It was another great exercise!

I found this all fascinating. This is often done with remote viewing where one can mentally "see" what others have seen and what is going on. We don't know if and what could be helpful being that one was a "cold case" from 1988.

I felt truly blessed and honored that we were even asked to try. It showed us how many ways our gifts can help others. It promotes healing in many ways. Being asked to help is an honor, individually and collectively.

Although not openly discussed, tapping in by those with metaphysical gifts is used by government and local law enforcement a lot. This is not anything new. In fact, it is written in history that great leaders employed "seers" to help them in their conquests. Participating in these exercises is the exciting part. Again, knowing you can make a difference is the key component.

There is something exciting about the process. The heartache around the circumstances though tug at my heartstrings at times too much. For others, it might not. Could I make a career out of doing this? It is not for me. I am willing to help when I am called to.

15

NINETY PERCENT ACHIEVER

G rowing up, my mom always labeled me a 90 percent achiever. Supposedly, I get almost to the very end of whatever task or challenge I am tackling and then give up. I didn't know I did this until she brought it to my attention. I thought it was a badge of honor to be able to walk away no matter what. She saw it differently, so I looked at myself through her eyes, as children often do, eventually. All I can say is, DANG!

I'm fighting to do that right now. My mom's words still ring in my head. My current challenge is to stay on the same hamster wheel or jump off and see what else is going to happen.

Although the stakes have been firmly nailed around the entire door of my past by *Moi*, I still have a hammer in my tool belt to take said nails out and go back.

Do I want to? OH, HELL NO! The one extremely strong message I have received repeatedly has been a warning from spirit. *If*

I even entertain returning to the past, I will take on others' karma. Do I know all the details of what said karma is? NOPE! Oh, but I have had dreams where spirit shows things to me that I will not even repeat here! I have heard in my readings and have had extremely vivid prophetic dreams of possible situations and instances that may happen. So, knowing what I know, is it even a sort of contemplation? If you saw what I saw and heard what I heard? That's a big NOOOOOOOO!

I am very much aware that going back to what is familiar and repetitive is the easy way out. Look around at people who take the "safe" route in life. That's what I'm talking about. I know what to expect from the people I have dealt with. Frankly, it's the same old same old. Lather, rinse, repeat.

What is nudging me forward is excitement, and freedom to make different and better choices. Funny how much better my back and shoulders are feeling since I took off the burdens placed on me by others. In fact, I have a neck again from much less stress! My job is to just contemplate what *I* want. No more people pleasing!

So, I am at 90 percent—standing at the crossroads of tomorrow and yesterday. Yesterday was a repeat of a movie I have watched a bunch of times. I know all the words and actions to it. It's scripted, repetitive, and predictable—sometimes with new players in familiar parts. I am armed now with more self-confidence, boundary-setting skills, lessons that have kicked my ass and a new understanding of how life works. I will stand in and defend my future first.

As I move forward to finally complete the last 10 percent, I will be leaving a bit more baggage here and there. It will be scattered.

Frankly, this baggage is opinions of what other people think I should do with my life, where I should go, and how I should live. I will also leave behind old habits and behaviors that have not served me in the past, but I have yet to replace with new ones. Along with these revelations, some people might part ways with me and that's OK.

I feel that spirit is moving and shifting things around to present options and opportunities to move forward. As I take steps forward, I will, in turn, have completed that last 10 percent. My mom will be proud of me!

I'm excited and scared all at the same time. I have argued that although the words *the world is your catalog* are ever-present, if you don't know all that there is, how can you know what you want?

All I know is how I *want* and *don't* want to feel. The fear of going back and repeating what I have already gone through *far surpasses* what I think the future holds for me. Thus, I embrace it with open arms. It will forever be better than where I was.

In warning though, be impeccable with your words and labels. Some might stick and will become a self-fulfilling prophecy.

So, *hear ye, hear ye! I declare I am no longer a 90 percent achiever— I am a 100 percent achiever!*

16

CHANNELED LECTURING

I have a friend who is at the beginning stages of putting herself back together again after dealing with a verbally abusive boyfriend. Quite honestly, she's not showing any signs that this last encounter was the final straw. I could be wrong, but I feel there is wavering. That didn't stop my gums from flapping to give her a pep talk. Spirit had something to say to her from me for sure!

She was strong enough to call me directly and explained she needed me to help her not go kiss and make up. She knew this was a bad idea. I agreed. What I really wanted to dig into was find out *why* she wanted to.

For the sake of argument, I will call her El*. El and I go way back. We have taken turns helping each other during different events that caused overthinking.

She has helped me to shift to a different consciousness at different times with recommendations of lectures or groups for what my needs were for the moment. No doubt, spirit channeled through her many times to help me. I do the same for her! We have this long-standing relationship where it doesn't matter who, what, where, or when we can call each other for a sympathetic ear or advice. The unspoken rule is we are tough on each other. No coddling. It is done out of love.

It was my turn to help her. She called and my mouth started running. I looked at the time and noticed we'd talked for about an hour. I don't lecture everybody who talks to me about everything, but she asked for help and my goodness, it was just unstoppable how fast everything came out of my mouth. Like, there were times I was talking, and I felt outside of myself looking on at the situation and wondering, *WHO ARE YOU?*

I caught myself saying some supremely profound things that I know darn well were not me! It was as if spirit said, "*Oh good, she's listening*" and tell her everything she needed to hear right then. *Anything* to keep her from going back to the man she finally broke away from.

I was trying to pick up the root cause of why she wanted to go back. All this involved shadow work for her. I really should dub this kind of direction "shadow-work-slang."

I asked her what she pictured of herself going forward. Asked what was *her* dream? Given she is an entrepreneur herself, I waited for a litany of her dreams. Her answer though? Helping this guy she just left with *his* business. I stopped her to say, "No, that is *his* dream. It's your support of *his* dream. Try again, what is *YOUR* dream?"

She hesitated and then admitted that she didn't know anymore. That is not characteristic of her *at all*.

DING DING DING DING!

If asked to repeat everything that I channeled to her, I couldn't. That's what happens when I channel. There were some parts where I felt disassociated with my voice as if I was a puppet.

So, despite me giving her the information that spirit was spewing from my loose lips, I wasn't convinced that she wasn't going back to this guy.

That's when I reminded her that I did it for many years and asked her if she was willing to give up another few years and repeat the cycle? Of course, she said no. It's amazing how much time slips by you before you finally hit the wall and say, enough is enough.

There is a generational history of like-kind situations in her family. I encouraged her to sincerely put forth the effort to heal. She needed to find the root issue, so she doesn't watch her daughter go through the same turmoil.

It was probably a good, solid hour of conversation with her. I felt shocked when I got off the phone though. Why? Well because of all the cool things I channeled! Spirit also brought to my awareness how much I have done to be where I am. I felt immense gratitude for all that had been accomplished. I hadn't looked at it like that before.

Do I have my PhD in all of this? No. I just see things differently now from the outside than from the maze she was still solidly in.

I really wanted to pat myself on the back. Every single little thing that she needed to start working on, consider or think about, I realized I had already done. It didn't happen overnight but over the span of a few years. My circumstances were also different. Healing is not a cut-and-dry five-step process either. It took several years but I did the work. There is a reason we were in each other's lives.

El is so amazing and helpful to many. I am honored that we help one another. I informed her that she was going to have a hell of a story to tell! Her story is going to help someone else.

No one gets to jump to the end of this inner shadow work. To break free, you must go through it. I swear, I tried every shortcut all leading to the same situation again and again.

I could hug her for patiently listening to me repeatedly in years past. Each time I tried to spin the circumstances differently like it would have made a difference. I lost count of how many times I swore I would never do it again only to put my rose-colored glasses on, throwing my hat back into the ring.

Anyway, I just wanted to spout off that I channeled a lecture. If she does the necessary work, I can see her moving mountains and making a further impact on many lives going forward. As of right now though, I question if she's going to give in. I pray she doesn't. She has been on this roller coaster with this guy for years now. She needed to do the internal healing not only for herself but also for the other generations of women in her life to come.

So, I spoke words that no doubt sound like a daunting task when you hear all the things that you've got to do in order to get to the other side. Regardless, I'm glad that I was there for her and that she called me. If nothing else, I hope that my experience will be a survival guide for her in the future.

I continue to stand next to her through this journey with grace and patience. It's not easy for anyone but it is definitely worth it.

17

TRYING OUT THE NEW ME

I went to the "school of life" and received quite an education. I have my diploma in hand. Have I used what I learned? A lot of it yes. Some of it, not yet.

It's like getting some cute outfits but not ever wearing them. Even though you think about wearing them, sadly, putting on the good-old stuff because it sounds, well, it's easier and predictable.

Habits die hard, they say. Right now, though, I am feeling book smart and street not-so-smart. Why? I have new skills and yet want to revert to some old ways.

I feel great! Mentally, I am back in shape. I know this because things that I forbade myself to do are now becoming OK to do again—but the right way.

That being said, there are still some old habits that I have that are front and center for me to address and I am fighting them off tooth and nail. They say you must replace an old habit with a new one. Well, I have been presented with another one to work on.

SPIRIT, GIVE ME STRENGTH!

You see, on my journey with a past person, someone once point-blank told me, "They are better at this game than you are." Wait, *what did you say?* That sounded like a challenge, not advice! I took that statement as a challenge and repeatedly got into the ring until I had enough bumps and bruises to never get back in.

They were, indeed, an expert at the games they played. Frankly they still are! Chances are slim that they are going to change. Why? It is all they know. It is their shields they put up. Years of studying people, and literally googling female weaknesses and strategizing how to capitalize on them for their own benefit. They would groom themselves to be exactly who you wanted. The masks they wore, along with what I also coined "their Rolodex" of pawns allowed them to always have a stake in the game. This was also their identity and way of life. It is and will probably forever be what they do to protect themselves. *HURT PEOPLE, HURT PEOPLE.* Their games, their rules, their triumph. As long as it makes them happy it is all they care about.

So, I admonished the fact that I would never play their games again. I took my card out of his Rolodex, my toys from the sandbox, and left. GAME OVER.

So, the old habit I am struggling with is to parade my new and improved life. This is an old habit *I* had in the past. I would leave the ex while we were dating, lick my wounds, and put myself back together again feeling better than ever! Then, I would make sure I was out and about appearing available to do it all over again. Wretched cycle! I know now, why I was doing it. Damn ego!

My actions were no longer an unconscious act. The gig was up. I stepped back and analyzed piece by piece and layer by layer what I wanted to do and why. It was important for me to figure this out. I did not want to go back ever again, so why was I wanting to do this?

Yup, this is not about them but once again about me. *I had to own this behavior.*

The sassy higher self in charge calls my ass out every time I even think about doing this stuff. I'm listening but frankly, some days it's hard. My ego is pleading with my higher self-exclaiming that my actions would be a "benefit."

My higher self-shouts back, *"GO SIT DOWN! Let me tell you exactly what you are doing: You are baiting that hook just to see if any of the old fish will follow it. Even though you don't want the fish, you want to know that you still got it. You are wanting to flaunt that bait in front of the fish then get upset when the fish swims around you."*

My ego hates being called out.

Tsk, tsk, tsk.

As spirit often does, they will put a statement in my path that is sometimes a smack up-side the head.

The latest one was: *Very few deserve to know about your life, how you are doing, where you are going, or what you have planned. Your ideas and dreams are not anyone else's business. Stay classy and stealth-like. It will get you so much further along than the way you had been doing it. You don't see the ulterior motives to derail you as we do.*

I took my power back and changed the internal tape. Taking the time to think and understand the reason why this old habit came up again, well, I can see how it would not be good for me. It was a habit I do not care to repeat.

This time, by not doing anything, I did it right!

18

SAGE AND TOILET PAPER

When you want things to happen and they do, it's only natural to want to keep the momentum going! Why not? I'm excited!

As they have done in the past, my angels have lined things up for me work-wise that will yield me the resources to get me out of the weeds. I am really happy about the potential of things that are coming—such great things! It does keep me really busy, and I do NOT mind!

I took a brief time-out to get a reading for myself. Just for the record, my brain was so busy I couldn't channel for myself. So, I made an appointment with someone. Now, considering that I run a woo-woo group and one of the things we do is exchange readings, you would think that I would get all the messages I would need from them. Not necessarily. Because we are so familiar with each other's stories, some things get glossed over. So, I have my standbys. I only see this particular lady maybe once or twice a year now. She doesn't know what's going on with me and she just knows to tell me like she sees it. Again, I always give the blanket permission slip to not sugarcoat anything. I want raw, blunt in-my-face statements, which is exactly how I need to hear it.

Technically speaking, it really wasn't a bad reading, but I just felt different because of how I received it. Was it all rainbows, butterflies, and unicorns? Oh, hell no! I always get new nuggets of things to chew on.

I have a personal rule that I don't listen to a reading I recorded for myself for at least a day or two. Well, I broke my own rule and listened again en route to a friend's house. So, I was a bit in my head.

I want to stress that I was in a woo-woo frame of mind but did not ask for a bubble of protection to be around me as I went inside my friend's house to pick something up. After all, it was just her, right? WRONG! Lesson learned!

I walked in and her extremely rambunctious dog was overly excited to see a visitor. He is a total sweetheart but was nonstop barking, probably sensing my angels around me! On top of that, her house echoes a lot. The TV was on, and the volume seemed to be very high. Everything was so loud! My friend, being used to all of this just talked *louder* to compensate.

At the moment it felt like a mental assault. On top of it, I felt some wonky energy. Something didn't feel right! Seriously, it was palpable to me! I was very overwhelmed and needed to leave, fast! Something-felt-off. I didn't know what, I just knew my visit was going to be short-lived. My soul was saying, *GET OUT OF THERE!* I have not felt like this before at her place, but I did that day.

So, I quickly told her goodbye and left. I felt like I was practically peeling out of her driveway to get away. I got maybe three houses down the street and spirit insisted that I needed to sage myself *RIGHT NOW.* I had to get whatever this bad juju energy was off me.

I always carry sage and a lighter in my purse. So, I stopped in the middle of the road just out of sight of her front door. There were no other cars on this residential street, so I put the car in park and dug the sage out of my purse and lit some. *OF COURSE*, as I do, a car turns the corner and is headed toward me. I needed to move my car out of the way. I do so while holding freshly lit sage. Talented, aren't I?

I waved this smoking sage around the car as much as I could while driving. No worries, there's just a little bit of embers and some smoke. Of course, with windows tinted, if I was pulled over, it would've been a typical scene from Cheech and Chong's *Up in Smoke.* Regardless, I say my words to remove any wonky energy. I drive forward, the car grows increasingly smokier, and I'm twisting and waving my arm backward to get the back seat of the car.

Just as I am making a contortionist move, the sage *gets caught on the twelve-pack of new toilet paper that I had bought earlier that day.*

Let's pause for a moment, shall we?

I have lit pieces of sage with golden embers, in a car filled with smoke, that has now landed on a brand-new pack of toilet *PAPER*, and I am so far into traffic that I can't pull over.

I'm continually glancing in my rearview mirror to the back seat to see if the toilet paper is going up in flames. I couldn't see anything, yet.

I just started hysterically laughing at the absurdity of it all, while still driving. What a story this was going to make! *"No, officer, I was not smoking in the car. I was saging while driving and the toilet paper caught on fire, I swear!"*

I then wondered if I would make the news and how the headline would read: *"Local woo-woo woman catches car on fire while driving. Embers from lit sage drop on toilet paper igniting car. Story at eleven!"*

I finally pulled over. No singe marks. Toilet paper is intact. I never found the stick of sage, but my car was not burning to the ground. *PHEW!*

Look, given the circumstances, I chalk this up to divine intervention. I don't know how else to explain this one! Seriously, never a dull moment! No doubt it did help to raise my vibration, get me out of my head and banish any negative juju that I felt I had around me not only from the sage but the laughter. I seriously felt the difference!

Note to self: No more lit embers in the car!

Dear Reader,

Every so often it would be good for you to wave some sage in your car to clear the energy in there. Residual energy from people you meet or places you have gone accumulate in there as well as your home. Just don't do it with a fresh pack of toilet paper in there!

19

WHAT LIES IN LIMBO

Remember SAT and ACT tests? Schools use them to see if you know everything that you were supposed to learn from your high school days so you can get into a good college! The higher the score, the higher the caliber of options you have! If you don't pass, it's OK because you just take a different path. Ultimately, we all end up living a life that we choose.

I have summarized that life is a series of lessons and tests. You keep taking the test until you have learned the lesson. Only then can you move on to the next thing to learn for your growth.

So, I was having a conversation with my girlfriend. I implied that I'm listening to and watching other friends date, but I am not ready to take the "final exam" to see if I have officially learned my lessons and have set appropriate boundaries.

I admit that I enjoy listening to everybody else and how they are doing. Frankly, it's fascinating! OK, it's the conservative, safe route.

Why? Because it is not *my* heart, time, or emotions! I like listening to stories, eating popcorn on the couch while my hair is up in a messy bun, no makeup on in yoga pants. Another way to say it is that I have no skin in the game!

Now, though, I'm thinking about this. It really struck a chord with me. What IS holding me back from taking a step forward?

See, spirit told me I have one more "test" before I move on. I think this is the equivalent of that massive final exam in college. Time is passing me by, and I don't seem to care. I know I am going to pass. Am I going to be nice about it? That I can't say with any assurance. Going forward would mean I must make decisions, get dressed, and show up.

I think that is the issue. It's about opening my heart and being vulnerable. I don't know what that looks like anymore. Like, I'm tired of all the unknowns. I don't want to play guessing games, wondering if someone is telling the truth, questioning their motives, and throwing my hat in the ring. Right now, all that is around me are past people. So why dip my toe in the water to swim? Besides, I have this cozy little safe area I have created. If I leave and come back, I might have new baggage. I don't want that.

OK, fine! It's fear. I need to work on this. UGH! I am calling this a personal time-out. I don't want to falter at all and then need to do all this work again.

I have reflected on the person I became during this last go-round, and it was *not* pretty! Ever hear of the saying if you want to find something out ask a woman? Well, let's just say I wear my junior detective badge with pride. It was well earned! I just don't ever want—no, I will NEVER do that again. So, if I don't date or go out much, then I can't get hurt, *right*? I'm not sure what I am going to do going forward. So herein lies where I currently am at, in limbo.

Limbo is a safe-but-stuck place. Mind you, I'm just talking about dating, but this could apply to anything, really! It's just being willingly stuck. Not moving forward or backward. Just "there."

I would like to declare that right now, I don't feel bad about this. But should I? Well, maybe. Time is flying by. The new rules that govern my life are in place. I just haven't tested them in the real world. In my eyes, they work. It could be the fear that going out again will bring up more things that I don't want to deal with.

Frankly, it's been a helluva upheaval and I can't say with 100 percent certainty that I am fully recovered. So, I listen from afar to others. Out of everyone so far, only my friend Canada has gotten it right. The rest of my friends? Well, they are back on the same merry-go-round again. Frankly that scares the crap out of me! What if I make a mistake?

I will get back out there again. When? I don't know. When I am ready, I won't even think twice. I'll hold my nose and jump into the deep end and doggy-paddle until I know what is going on. For now, I have other things going on that have my attention, which has been my excuse.

I have been warned that the time is drawing near for this last "test." I even got permission to be firm and burn the bridge! (Imagine that, spirit is giving me permission! HA!) They want to make sure that I don't opt for the old merry-go-round with the same damn horses.

The next section in my schooling is a new set of people, lessons, and experiences. Funny that I can see a lot of them moving into place and that time is near. I have to trust myself to make the right decisions. I don't know if that is possible without a cheat sheet. This time I will have my gifts in full force and can lean on my trusted counsel of spirits. This will be different for me in the dating realm.

Just for the record, we are never done with lessons. Life is a school. It doesn't matter what the subject is. There will be a time that if I don't jump in willingly, I will be shoved.

For now, I hover and sit in the in between of limbo.

20

The Rabbit Hole of Spirituality

Learning about all things spiritual is fascinating. The more you learn and see your gifts develop, the more you want to know. It's like a drug that feeds your soul. I think that is why they call it an awakening. It feels no less thrilling than ripping open the curtains and letting the sunshine in!

Then, there are the coolest clair-toys you get developing your spiritual gifts. It is mind-blowing! There is clairsentience (clear feeling), clairaudience (clear hearing), clairvoyance (clear seeing), clair cognizance (clear knowing), and clairalience (clear smelling).

I want to stress that I have never been "religious." I came from a family that was born into but not practicing Catholicism. When my stepfather came into the picture, we traveled from church to church. He needed the constant adoration achieved by attending a new establishment. (He was a narcissist.) So when the latest church-of-the-moment caught onto his antics, we changed religious institutions again. When asked, I always told everyone that I have been every religion except Hindu and Buddhist. Mind you, I found peace everywhere we attended but didn't always agree with all the rules or scare tactics. Something inside me just didn't find one catch-all truth. When I was old enough to label myself, I just said I was a believer and spiritual. This usually avoided the debates and potential arguments of well-meaning folks trying to convert me to their side of the fence.

Now, finding out what I have thus far makes so much sense to me. I feel at home, and I feel free. I am spiritual.

At times, you can get so wrapped up in learning about angels and your personal spirit team and guides that you forget you are human. You must live your life, make mistakes, and be vulnerable.

I also had the gift of time for a while to look up, read, ask, and feed all of my desires to learn and grow more of what I was attracted to. Computer research made it easy to read others' opinions and their scope of knowledge. Classes on interests I had helped me learn. No one knew me, so I could just be nosey and the question queen. Then, experience has helped me grow.

At times though, being spiritual can become a crutch. Sadly, that happened to me. Actually, it still does every so often.

I was so excited that I could ask for signs and angels would tell me! I was feeling so content and connected that, after a while, I had an awareness that I suddenly couldn't make a decision on my own without asking.

Someone coined this "analysis paralysis." There was an underlying fear that crept in that I didn't even realize.

As unhappy as I had been for the last few years, happiness was my drug of choice. Doing all that I was doing, I felt I had a direct connection to it. I did not want the feeling to go away. If I always asked angels about everything, the answer would always be right! Therefore, I will never be wrong. If I am never wrong, then I won't be unhappy. I didn't want to feel bad or do anything that wasn't perfect. So, I asked my new BFFs about *everything*! TA-DA! Drum roll please! I had figured life out! Woo-hoo!

That is, until my everyday questioning didn't work anymore. I got cut off. Just enough to get my attention. My plans weren't working out. The signs weren't showing up. Oh, if there was a customer service department for my spirit team, I was *so* trying to find it! *What did I do wrong that I got cut off? Tell me? I'll fix it and we can go right back to the way things were!* Why were they mad at me and not talking to me through signs anymore?

Yup, the air was let out of my tires, and I came to a screeching halt. I searched for answers.

Then I channeled. The message was that I was using it as a crutch. I needed to use my other gifts like my intuition and my other "clairs." You see, I have all of them and like any muscle, I needed to strengthen them. I needed to pause and feel into the energy so I can do this on my own, anywhere, at any time. As Glenda the Good Witch said, "*You had the power all along, my dear.*"

So, spirit took off my training wheels without warning and made me ride the bike alone. Damn if I wanted to! It most certainly forced muscles into shape that I needed to strengthen. It took work, effort, and time. It wasn't hard work. I just didn't have the master cheat sheet anymore to just get the answers right. I fumbled. I had to make mistakes!

I am not alone. This has happened to other woo-woo friends too. Therefore, I am mentioning it in case it happens to anyone else. Even one of my teachers in England said that she thought she was just sailing along, then was, as she described, "cut off." They wanted her to strengthen her *other* gifts. When she did, her main ones came back.

During an exchange in the beginning, I was told in no uncertain terms that if I didn't quit using my oracle cards as a crutch instead of channeling during readings, they were going to cut me off.

Jeez! Alright already! Message received.

Spirit doesn't play!

There is so much differing information that it is easy to get caught up in it all and lean on them for help.

I am a very independent thinker for the most part, but I get tired. I don't want to play the guessing game as to whether it is the right answer or not. I just want the open-book test where I can look up the answers. I would prefer the red phone direct to the angels. I have pleaded with them at times for them to just tell me what to do. Does it happen? NOPE!

There are many reasons your soul has come to this earth. Most of it is to learn. How do you learn and grow if you don't do it on your own? Yes, we all have free will. I am very willing to just follow along and do everything right to avoid conflict and feeling bad. My spirit team will not let me.

It took me a really long time to figure this out, so I thought I would save you some time by sharing. Practice, learn, ask questions, and agree to grow. Most of us on this journey of life have more than one gift. If you don't work on the other ones, spirit will find a way to infuse them into your life, but you will have to practice.

Being a spirit junkie is easy. As I told someone this past weekend, spirit doesn't mind you trying to learn them all, but every gift is not cookie cutter and will work differently for you. Try and do too much and they will hold some back, as they are the next step. They all build on one another. It has been my experience that spirit will gift you knowledge to work on one, maybe two gifts at a time.

We are not supposed to know everything that's going on, despite our valiant effort. Obviously, I didn't get in the correct lane for the lazy river rafting trip of life either. I continue to grow, expand, and learn. They make me slow down to learn despite my efforts for the crash course and wanting to rush through it all. Now, I have more than a few things to learn. One step at a time.

My advice: Don't be afraid. It is a crazy ride but very much worth it!

21

PAST "COMPLIMENTS" THAT REALLY WEREN'T COMPLIMENTS

"How did you get someone like her?"

So, I'm helping Agent 007 do some yard work. I wanted to help because I feel such gratitude for everything that she has done for me. I haven't worked in a yard since I sold my house and moved to North Carolina. My head and heart thought it was a great idea to help, but my body, not so much. The tunes were on. The sun was out, and we were both tackling the various landscaping projects. It felt good to dig in the dirt.

Let me just politely say that my cardiovascular and my resistance are way lower than they've ever been. Agent 007 though is right up there with the Energizer Bunny. I want to clarify that her Energizer Bunny status is not a single 9V battery. She's like a car battery with lots of power! The woman does not stop!

Despite me trying to hold my own, she ran circles around me. My efforts seemed so sad in comparison to hers. It reminded me that I, too, have been like her for a long, long time. I used to idle at seventy-five miles per hour. It's how I used to roll! When I moved, it came to a screeching halt. I went from all the responsibilities of a homeowner to an apartment and flipping the light switch on and off.

As I was watching her just go-go-go, it reminded me that I was like this! It definitely looks a little different from the outside in. Then spirit reminded me of a "compliment" that people said of me many times to my ex-husband.

"How did you ever get someone like her?"

It was in reference to how much and how fast I used to work. I was that person who did my stuff and everyone else's.

So many examples of this started flooding the peanut gallery of my thoughts. My brain drew lines in the sand and had a battle royale while I worked.

Was this really a compliment? Spirit encouraged me to look deeper into this.

The Cliffs Notes version is that I was like Agent 007. I loved doing all the stuff I could do and then half the stuff my other half was doing as well, all with little to no recognition for all that was being done. For some reason, I felt like this was just some sort of badge of honor.

As a child I somehow adopted the thought that if I was to receive any love, acknowledgment, or respect, it was "expected" that I was to give 500-plus percent. If you had an extra five minutes, there was something you should have been doing! Anything less was not good enough.

Don't you love trauma responses? NOT!

There were occasions when people tried to help me. I just felt that if I didn't do it myself it would be used against me. I would then be further labeled that I couldn't handle something and would be less-than. So of course, I not only had to be Superwoman but Superman. This was my self-imposed penance to pay for love and acceptance.

Some of this also came from watching females in my life. I didn't want to end up like them, having to deal with unsavory situations because they needed help. Oh, the web we weave.

Again, I can't tell you how many times people said this in my presence while with my ex. They weren't shy about it either. They would just come up and say, "*How did you get someone like her?*" Of course, I took this as a sincere compliment because I was obviously now "doing enough" to impress even my extended friends and family. Finally, I was "good enough." Finally, I had found the magic formula that would make someone else see my value and worth. Finally.

Yep, a real winner …

Now I see that this was not a compliment anymore. At different phases of your life, you only hear things that seem to stand out and that are important.

In my defense, I was trying to receive recognition, to stake my claim in my family and among my friends that I could hold my own and do it all. I felt the need to prove that I was not a burden or needy. And they let me, because I was stubborn.

There was a commercial I heard once whose lyrics were: "*I can bring home the bacon, fry it up in a pan, and never let you forget you're the man ...*" Again, this is what I felt I *had* to do. Nobody forced me, I just felt I had to do it. I didn't see value in myself. I looked for it in others. Unless they said something aloud. My efforts weren't good enough.

Sadly, my interpretation at the time was that I was only great because of everything I did and only if it was vocalized. I made exceptional money, and paid for most everything myself without needing to lean on any additional resources. I took great pride in everything I did, every place I went, and still managed to do everything. Only in exhaustion I felt it was finally enough.

These actions were also breeding more codependency. Everyone let me be this way. I wouldn't and couldn't allow anyone to help me. I was the Energizer Bunny on steroids and proud of it.

I think some of this was compounded by my adolescence and self-worth. Rarely did someone compliment me. In my eyes that told me that I still wasn't good enough. I didn't give enough. I didn't do enough, basically, I wasn't enough for anybody. No one thought I was that great. I had no worth. I felt I was a burden and a waste of space. I looked for value from others. I tried harder, worked more, gave more, and tried to stand out. Finally, when someone would ask, "*How did you get someone like her?*" I thought I was FINALLY good enough for them, but no one tried to steal me away and make me theirs. I now see one of my love languages is words of affirmation.

Oh, what I have learned. I find it so sad that it has taken me this long to know all this. Have I really lived with my head in the sand all this time?

I've chosen to get off the hamster wheel. Now I only take on what is my responsibility, and I don't take on the responsibilities of others. I also am not trying to impress anyone. I know my worth, I know what I bring to the table, and I don't have to do circus tricks anymore to prove it. PERIOD!

I finally realized that when people would say, "*How did you get someone like her?*" it wasn't that I wasn't good enough for them but that they couldn't keep up with or find someone like me *to do everything for them.* It wasn't that I didn't do enough. *I did way too much.* That was their way of acknowledging that I was giving some people in my life a free ride with all the glory and a lot less of the work.

It goes back to a friend reminding me that just because I chose to do something the hard way and take it all on myself, doesn't mean I did it better. Sadly, that's true.

I am very much aware now of an equal exchange of energy. I have exhausted myself to the point of realizing that if I need help, I need to ask. I'm still not good at it but I have been a student of this lesson for many years and will continue to be.

I look back at that time and realize that I ran with other friends at the same level as myself. Agent 007 being one of them. It was fun to see how much more we could put on our plates. Funny, the only people who we impressed were each other.

Maybe it was exhaustion, dehydration, or the hot sun while working that made me think about all of this. Years and years have taught me a lot. Pausing has allowed me to give thought and listen to my soul.

I honestly could die today and feel like I have done so much and have no regrets. Everyone is running their own race. There are still quite a few people looking for someone to do their work for them. I can spot them a mile away now. Well, that's not going to happen with me. Call me a little bit hardened but from now on, if somebody says how did you get someone like her, I'm going to hold my head up high. It's with dignity and respect for myself. It is no longer because of how much I did for someone else, but how much I do for me.

Dear Reader,

If there is a past memory that pops up along your journey take the time to look at it further. There is often an example or a lesson to learn that spirit wants you to look at again that you couldn't have seen being in the moment.

22

BINGO!

Agent 007 and I went to play bingo at the community clubhouse in her new development for something to do on a Friday night. We were armed with different colored sheets, blotters, our favorite beverage, and snacks. We were determined to win!

Unfamiliar with the people in her community, I took a few minutes to look around. In MY opinion, Agent 007 and I were by far the youngest people playing that night. We both agreed that there was probably some very suspect content in the Tervis tumblers of those at the rowdy table.

At our table, there was a lovely lady who sat with us. If I could profile her by looks alone, she presented herself as a secretary who lived strictly by the rules, had 2.5 kids, and a house in the suburbs.

In making small talk, though, she told Agent 007 and me that she was a recent transplant from another state, and she was bored.

Without skipping a beat, she also mentioned that she told her husband that she was either going to get a part-time job or **have an affair.** (I did not misquote her either!) I practically choked on my drink.

She said that her husband opted for her getting a part-time job and she also had a red Mustang convertible. As an empath, I am used to people divulging their life story at the most random times, but it certainly was a first to have someone haphazardly just blurt out that the only choices in her life were a job or an affair! It was like someone saying, I-AM-PREGNANT-PASS-THE-BUTTER. Coincidentally then, bingo started, and I was trying to digest what she said and also pay attention. This was a two-minute conversation and she said all of this! Looking back, I wonder if it was a diversion tactic!

Just for the record, despite all my gifts, I don't get any free passes for lottery numbers or bingo games. I'm just saying.

Anyway, between her comments and the random participants yelling BINGO, I found myself looking around the room. I mean REALLY looking. The cornucopia of diversity around me felt profound. What stood out is that everyone had a story. Everyone presented themselves as someone else when they were younger that is different from now.

I looked at the roomful of men and women. When some spoke, you could tell there was a toughness in them, but everyone's bodies gave way to who they were now. Your body is not who your soul is. It's just the suit your soul resides in while here on earth.

In my profession, I have met many people over the years and when I have asked them what their professions were, I am often astonished. *NEVER* would I have guessed. Why? Because it's not who they are anymore. *IT'S WHO THEY WERE.* Some still leaned on their profession as a badge of honor and some simply knew that their profession was what they DID, but not who they were anymore.

Many of the people around me in bingo were probably teenagers in the 1950s or '60s. They probably had firm bodies, attitudes, and slicked-back hair, talking about whether to go to park somewhere or find the car races. Now? Molded and shaped by their life experiences, most are in stretchy clothes, with short hair and not-so-tough exteriors. Life has humbled many and they don't look so tough anymore, yet they are full of stories and life lessons. Time has a way of forcing a metamorphosis. Like it or not we all shed who we try to stay like and evolve.

I realized that these people all have had more than a few trials, tribulations, and triumphs. They all carry many secrets. We are all molded by the lessons that we learn and don't learn, the resolve we acquire, and the patience to allow others to be who they are and not who we think they should be. It's the gift we get to open as we get older.

The toughness that many of these people have worn as armor in their life has given way to congeal into who they are today.

I'm getting ready to attend a high school reunion and question if there is enough duct tape to mold my body back to the way it was in high school. There isn't. (I did try that once, but that's another story.) Of course, there are those who have maintained the appearance that they are exactly the same—and yet they are not. Most have fought battles no one knows about, yet we all try and turn back the hands of time and fake the fact that we are still the same. Yet, we are not.

Life will mold and shape us. We are always changing and evolving. Some put up a fight, but life will win.

I know *I* am not the same. I love learning who you were, and who you have become. Everyone has a story!

I realize now that some people stay stuck in the past. They are afraid to step forward. YESTERDAY was always better. The current moment would never hold a candle to what already happened.

I was with someone who used this as a crutch. It is almost like they were in a time warp of *yesterday*. *WHY*? They know what happened, what to expect and how to deal with it. It is sad that they can't live in the moment and appreciate what is going on currently. They hold on to the past like it is going to come back again.

Not understanding this concept for many years, I look back and realize that my people-pleasing ways had been fighting an unspoken battle to make today better than whatever this "yesterday" was. I learned that no matter how hard I tried or whatever I did, yesterday was *always* going to be better for this person. Old music, movies and stories.

I NOW know differently. It had nothing to do with me personally although inadvertently I became part of that landscape of yesterdays in this person's story as well.

We are all held accountable to step forward. It's the unknown and sometimes it's downright scary.

Our higher and truer selves come to the forefront as we get older and wiser. We start out being exactly who we are as children, only to be molded and stripped of our identities to conform to societal influences. Then we spend so much time trying to figure out who we truly are. Most often, we listen to our soul's calling. Piece by piece and layer by layer we unwrap all that has happened in our lifetime and work to clear out what no longer serves us. The new goal is to do what is best for us. Sacrifices have been made in the past and now we are doing what makes us happy.

Anyway, I didn't win any BINGO games but in between took a good look around at all the people in the same room. They honored themselves by doing what they wanted at the moment and that was trying to win as well.

No two journeys are alike. The wisdom you cannot see, though, is invaluable.

Dear Reader,

There is an old saying that the richest place on earth is the cemetery. There are stories, lessons, and so many ideas that never get passed on to those who might need it. Take the time you can to visit with those experienced individuals and learn from them. Talking to them will be good for everyone.

23

REALIZING LIFE BACKWARD

Spirit nudged me to get a reading for myself. When I asked from whom, the answer was to reflect on what has already been given to me. They suggested that I find wisdom and inspiration from words and messages already given.

So, I looked back at my book. A *book,* you ask? Oh, let me tell you about my book!

Just for the record, I record all the readings done for me. In fact, I've even transcribed them and put them in a notebook for faster reference for myself. Let's just call it a hobby of mine that has paid off in more ways than one.

When I do readings for other people, I offer to record their reading for them as well since it has helped *me.* I will give an example to prove my point. Spirit may hint at the sock holding six $100 bills that fell behind the dryer. Instinctively, as a sitter, you become fixated on that sock, where it came from, who put the money in there, and why you didn't notice it! In the meantime, though, spirit mentioned lottery officials knocking at your door on Tuesday at 3:06 p.m. They further add that you need not go down Willow Street because there's going to be a pothole that will break your axle. Then they mention to make sure that your hair is fixed because you are going to be discovered by a talent scout while having coffee on Thursday. All those details are just as important to you, but our brain becomes fixated on one thing, and we've skipped over the others. It's an elaborate description but true!

It's also about how the message is spoken, the voice inflection, and not paraphrasing but relaying exactly what was said. I have learned many personal lessons regarding this over the years. Thus, I have chosen to record them for my own benefit.

Now, mind you, there have been times that I don't like what I am hearing when a reading is done for me. Why? Because I am human. It also could have been the clarification of how a situation was going to go that was not how *MOI* wanted it to be. Do the readers ever notice this about me? NOPE! Oh, I have been told more than once I am a hard person to read. I always ask for raw, blunt, in-your-face, no-sugar-coating readings. Then, I am stoic as I receive the message. I realize that some patrons don't like to receive messages like that, I personally do. If I didn't say it before, let me tell you, no one can put a pair of rose-colored glasses on faster than my brain and spin its own version. My inner child always wants to hear about rainbows, butterflies and unicorns. Oh my! Alas, I type out the messages I record verbatim, so I don't twist what was said. I even have my own method of accentuating words and phrases so when I reread it, it reads like it sounded when it was given to me. I have sought out readers who talk this way for me. Not all will. It's not in their character. I get it.

Suggestion #1: Always ask permission but try and record your reading.

Suggestion #2: Find a reader who speaks like you want to hear. Soft or raw. Your choice.

Suggestion #3: Wait a day or two before relistening.

At times, I am so frustrated about what I think was said to me that I miss a lot of other key components. So, my standing rule has always been that once I get a reading, I let it digest. I try to not relisten for at least two days. Then I can relisten to it with fresh ears and dissipated emotional angst that I might have been feeling. After that, I type it up and put it in my handy-dandy notebook.

So, let's just say I've got a very healthy notebook of messages given to me in readings that I have received over the years. Call it a small hobby of things I collect. At times, it was spiritual therapy. There were hints and directions of ways I needed to look at further that were given to me. Mostly though, the urgency to look at myself. My therapists are my loved ones like my grandfather, grandmother and great-aunt on the other side as well as guardian angels and spirit guides. I just knew I was heard. I also appreciated the heads-up of things to come.

So going back and relistening to some of the messages that I have been given has been really interesting! I even have marked what has happened. Some messages didn't come to fruition for about two years, but they were no less important.

I channel messages for myself as I do for others. I record what comes out of my mouth as it is a reading for me. Relistening to myself has given me a moment of pause about how far I have come. I have lots of gratitude! Things that were once an issue are no longer. My mindset that was once one way, is now another. Oh, how my mindset has changed.

Listening or reading back, I could hear the desperation and frustration in my voice at times as I asked questions of other readers. I also learned that I talked a lot instead of listening! It is just a reminder to myself that when I do readings for other people, I do not ask for any explanation. Less is more.

Suggestion #4: Don't feed the reader! If you have a subject, present it. Don't tell a story. Spirit will tell you what you need to hear, not necessarily what you want to hear.

What I think is really interesting is hearing my questions about things at the beginning of my journey. I heard what made me scared and unsure at the time. I lacked trust and faith in myself. I also heard the things that have blossomed, bloomed, and expanded like new talents and ideas. Oh, how times have changed!

It's just really cool stuff!

Another thing I realized in rereading my transcribed readings is that every person I spoke to gave me one or two pieces at a time of the "puzzle" of life events. They say when the student is ready, the teacher will appear. Yeah, yeah, yeah.

Suggestion #5: Don't count on a line-for-line manuscript on how to live. You still have to do the work and all you get are hints.

I had my favorite go-to readers that gave me the dirt on things that I really wanted to know. Then there were others I was led to but didn't know the reason until they spoke. I just knew I was to get another puzzle piece of information.

Readers kept mentioning my wheelhouse of talents that I possessed. Frankly at the time I didn't believe them, yet every different reader told me about the same things over and over again.

At times, when I asked which way was up, spirit would only tell me which way was left. If I asked to know about specific things, I was told about nonrelated things. I think in the beginning they catered to my whims and my insatiable need for knowing. Then they worked to derail my efforts and get me more focused on myself and my gifts.

Often, I just scratched my head questioning why. I found no relevance in my moment of sitting there. Now? I know that different people speak using their veil of experience. Spiritual readers were directed to tell me what they did, if for no other reason than to plant a seed for me or for future reference of something unfolding for me. They were put in my path to relay messages that are meant for me in the way I needed to hear it at the time but didn't know it.

Suggestion #6: The messages you get could be for the future. Don't listen thinking it's all right now.

Whether I was intentionally or unintentionally paying attention at the time of the reading I appreciate the recording. Going back has allowed me to appreciate the information and value it differently than I would have at the time.

Reflecting on the readings I have received, I occasionally look back and admit that spirit and the information were right. Your life does not take just one route. The information you get in readings is for numerous scenarios that could play out should you take a certain direction. For example, moving to North Carolina was told to me. Also going to Arthur Findlay College in England. It's only when you look back that you realize you were indeed given the information. Then as time goes on, you realize how they were right about a lot more than what you even knew. I just know that the more you stay in touch with your spirit guides, the more you also learn what they could mean.

We can't fault ourselves. The bottom line is that we *all* only have knowledge up to what we learned yesterday. We don't know about tomorrow. (Although damn if I haven't tried!) It's guesswork. The goal is to take what you learned yesterday and move forward with it.

Suggestion #7: YOU HAVE FREE WILL. No one has all the answers except you.

There was one person who gave me a complete rundown of all the different gifts that I was going to have. Part of me just stared at them, incredulously thinking, *What the HELL are you smoking?* I sound like a wizard! Despite my human side feeling like they were blowing a lot of smoke in my direction, there *was* this other part that was on the edge of my seat, practically foaming at the mouth saying, *tell me more*! Actually, it explained a lot about myself that I didn't quite understand at the time, but boy, I do now!

So much of what I have been told has come to fruition thus far. I am always and will forever be a work in progress. I look for the finish line yet there is always another carrot. If I knew it all from the start, I wouldn't have some of these really cool stories to tell!

I do listen to whatever is told to me with a grain of salt. I question everything, as we ALL should. I sit with it. Hey, I am pretty stubborn at times. Just because it was said in a reading doesn't mean I'm instantly doing it or reacting to it. We all have free will. We all make mistakes. Of course, there are plenty of well-meaning people along the way who think they know what is best for you. I always remind people that I have yet to see a baby being born with a how-to manual slid between their ass cheeks. The rules of their existence are not in the imaginary book. We're *all* just trying to figure it out.

It's also a very sincere reminder that some things aren't meant for you to hear or learn until it's time. Oh, there were MANY times I just needed to know certain things and didn't get what I wanted. I always got what I needed.

It's also another strong reminder that you can't do the work for somebody else. All you can do is show them the next step or tell them the options to move forward.

Somebody might sit down in front of you and say, "Fix me, tell me what to do." I have done this myself over the years. I asked many questions of other people. It's hard when you must give that same message to somebody else and just explain it's up to you to figure this out for your growth. I'm only noticing and realizing a lot because I looked back and re-digested what was told to me through spirit.

Suggestion #8: You can't rush. What is meant to happen, will. (I have tried to rush, and it doesn't work.)

Suggestion #9: You cannot do the work for someone else. It's truly up to them.

My book of readings has been almost a sort of diary of my life through my spiritual journey. There is still more to write. Each reading has given me a puzzle piece to my story and the many *zillion* ways it can go. Only by looking back can I see how they fit together. I still do not have the full story. It is still unfolding. I am grateful and truly forgot about a lot of the nuggets of wisdom and explanations gifted to me. In fact, a lot was currently happening as I reread/listened. Once again, spirit was right to ask me to reflect. I didn't need a new reading to talk about tomorrow. I already had a reading about today.

24

Not My Monkey, Not My Circus

Lately, I have been in the spiritual class called *boundaries*. Boy, I am learning a lot these days! This part of the boundaries lesson is differentiating what is my issue or circumstance and what is someone else's. I have had to look long and hard as to where they end, and I begin, and what issues are mine to solve versus what belongs to someone else.

Mind you, as a recovering compulsive people pleaser, this is not as easy as it may seem. If you looked up "fixer" as a subcategory of people pleasing, I would be in there. I am the poster child.

I know the reasons for all of this but that's an entirely different lesson I had to learn as well. But back to boundaries. There are many different applications this word applies to, and this was just one subcategory. Spirit is making sure that this subject and examples of it are front and center for me to see. I am grateful. I have a lot to learn.

To start, my messages from spirit warned me of potential events that could happen. Of course, there are twenty different storylines. Which one will it be? Who knows! BUT! When the storyline or subject comes up in my oracle cards and dreams, I pay attention even more.

I've been getting a lot of what spirit is calling "events" that are going to happen. When there is a storm, it does not involve me, but it affects me. During moments of doubt or overthinking, I repeat this over and over—IT DOES NOT INVOLVE ME.

You would think I was handed a baton at a track meet. Holy hell, my mind was racing in overdrive on this one futuristic message. It didn't help that my dreams were showing me examples of this but metaphorically. Of course, at times, I took the dreams literally. Either way, spirit had my undivided attention.

One of the dreams was of me in a car driving through an intersection into a wall of rain. The car skidded, barely missing other cars until I was on the other side. I was fine. I can look at that as the rain and other cars were the "events" and I navigated my way out. I was never "involved" (crashed) but it was indeed harrowing. I was only responsible for my car and my safety.

How's that for a metaphor?

Another dream was seeing myself after being told of something about someone else that was so outrageous that it AFFECTED me but did not involve me. I literally watched myself as I received the news. I had no clue what it was, but my mouth was agape.

So, I paused and thought about what was going on around me. There was, indeed, turmoil for others and situations around me. Although I was told about them and was held back from participating or helping, there were indeed many storms that affected me but didn't involve me.

The office I worked out of in Florida was going through great upheaval and turmoil. There was a changing of the guard, new rules, new favoritism that affected me but did not involve me. I was not there to see it firsthand but heard about it and made further decisions because of it.

Some friends were having health issues. This affected some of my plans but did not involve me. My son's house was having work done to it and considering that is where I stayed, it was his issue to deal with. It didn't involve me but affected where I stayed when I was in town.

It just seemed that everyone around me had "stuff" going on. Not me, though. Some things affected me. I became acutely aware of what I needed to do to not become involved. It was a huge challenge for me at times. Remember, I am a recovering people pleaser. I had to practice NOT being available to listen to every little last detail of someone's strife. I had to actively practice not taking over the projects of others because I knew how to do something different or better.

I want to stress that sometimes I had to bite my tongue hard. The will to put whatever was going on with them onto my shoulders was stronger than I thought. I had to make a conscious effort to NOT do it. Those were examples of boundaries. There were some instances where I felt directed to step in and help in one way or another, but they were fewer and far between.

I think it shocked me just how much I was a human DOING instead of a human being. It also made me think about some standout moments that flooded back into memory and how often I have done this in the past. No wonder my stress levels were through the roof!

I admit, I was foaming at the mouth on some occasions because it just isn't my nature to sit back. I love to help but it has almost always been of detriment to myself in some way, shape, or form.

It felt good that these instances came up and I "practiced," but after having a revelation of achievement, I had questions.

Was this it? This was the storm? This was what my little pop quizzes were about? The answer from spirit was "NO." They proceeded to show me more dreams then. This time, more specific scenarios, situations, and the people involved. THOSE were worthy of the label STORMS. Ugh. The only thing I didn't get was the timeline for these. I continue to remind myself that they will affect me but will not involve me.

I am on the lookout for these bigger situations. I continue to practice these little baby steps of stepping back, not being everyone's dumping ground, and learning to not involve myself. It's not been a cakewalk. It's more of a practice run.

I have learned how much less drama and strife I have in my life because of this! I have learned to see when others want to give away their responsibility to others to deal with. I see things now with new eyes, compliments of spirit.

Am I going to make mistakes? YES. Spirit has also warned me to steel my backbone because there will be some very compelling conversations coming forth as to why something needs my involvement. They also warned me that setting boundaries and not participating will be a very unpopular decision but to stick to my guns and speak my truth.

I hope these trial runs were enough!

25

PATIENCE & PAYING ATTENTION

Readers often tell me that I manifest things all the time. Unfortunately, due to my fast-moving life and lack of patience, I have forgotten what I asked for if it doesn't show up in five minutes. I chalk it up that I must not deserve it and then quickly focus on the next thing I want. I wish someone had told me from the beginning that *manifesting does not always come with a magic wand that if I say something it will just appear or happen.* Seriously if it doesn't happen in five minutes, I must not be doing it right or it's not meant to be. So, NEXT!

I've been told for years that I am a master manifester. (Still chewing on that statement.) Of course, what I think that means is having access to a genie in a bottle at the snap of my fingers. In my mind, anything I touch will turn to gold. REAL gold. I imagine that everything I pick up or try to do is an instant success. (I swear I can see my angels laughing at all of this.) Is this the case? OH, HELL

NO! Spirit found a way to bring this subject to my attention. My angels put things in front of me to reflect on a lot.

Lesson time! I think they want me to see and reflect on how they have been helping and lining things up. Like, a lot of things, but because I don't pause long enough, I miss them. They have been doing this for me for years. I just never knew it. I bring this up because if you also pause and think back, you may see for yourself how this has been the case for you as well.

Spirit likes to pull up the memory reel in my head. It is so random when they do this! It's helpful to show me these selective moments so that I understand. They started with a trip down memory lane.

It started with the memory of being a teenager and attending a new high school after we moved. I had a list of fourteen whole things that I wanted in a boyfriend. I got everything I wanted!

I wanted a job; I got a job. I didn't really know what exactly I was doing but in some unknowing way, I could get what I wanted. I adopted a mantra that has served me well. "If I want it bad enough, it will always happen. It's a DONE DEAL."

I wanted a specific car, and my first car was exactly the car—complete with holes in the floorboard and all! I didn't care, *I GOT EXACTLY WHAT I WANTED*. Cheerleading team? YUP!

Did I ever have to wait for any of this? YES! OFTEN! It still didn't stop me, though, from having blind faith that it would happen or come to me. It just always did. I didn't know how or why at the time.

Funny, I feel like by not understanding, things happened faster because I got out of my way. I just accepted that when it was meant to be, it was going to be. Now, of course, I know what I'm saying, and I understand the process 1,000,000 percent more. Now, I have zero patience. I'm ready to go! I'm on the bandwagon! Let's get to manifesting!

Along with this gift came the heavy burden of childhood programming of how I must give ten times more to receive. There is a difference between an equal exchange of energy and not having to do anything in order to receive the one thing—whatever that was at the moment. I didn't know the difference then, but I do now! An equal exchange of energy is receiving as much as you are giving. For example, a friend who only calls you to dump their frustrations out on you but never seems to be available when you need to vent is an example of an *unequal* exchange of energy. Basically, when you are the one doing all the work or putting in the effort (giving) in a friendship or relationship, well that is what unequal is. It shouldn't be that way.

I've always been goal-driven because there was something I did or knew unconsciously that made things happen. Whatever I was doing, well, things happened for me.

I tried putting my fate for manifestation into someone else's hands. That *NEVER* produced the results I could. That was a big lesson to learn. I have learned to never hand that life choice over to anyone ever again.

I'm a little tornado when I want stuff done. Like, it is a done deal! Well, most of the time. I have my blinders on, energy super-charged, so wind me up and let me go!

There are times, though, that I feel like I've been put on the side of a highway on the shoulder of the autobahn and had to watch life zoom by. For whatever reason, I had no gumption to do anything. I now realize that there is a reason for everything but, at that moment, I didn't have a complete understanding of the reason why.

Spirit also reminded me of my energy capabilities! Some vacations landed me in Las Vegas. Slot machines were my game. I used to announce to everyone that I was feeling for "chi." I would put my hands up and walk by slot machines. If one felt energetic, I put my quarters in. I wasn't picky if I won fifty cents or five hundred dollars. Dead serious! I was just so excited because I could literally put my hands up and walk by slot machines and something would hit me like a nudge. I would put a couple of quarters in and would win something. I would travel from machine to machine to machine. I have a routine and a system, led by (unknowing) intuition. No one could touch me, though. I just needed to be left alone to roam the casino.

I prayed and begged the heavens to ONLY have boys when we were ready to have kids. I did, indeed, have only boys. Now I look back though—did my desire and manifestation have anything to do with this?

I have made vision boards and have acquired items pictured on them. They work!

The more I have learned, the more amazed and astounded and grateful I have become. I think that is the reason for spirit's trip down memory lane with me. I never really realized until after the fact that I had a lot of "thank-yous" to catch up on!

Fast forward through life and you'll notice that there are some cute, meaningful things that have happened here and there. I'm always astounded but don't talk about them. Mostly because I am always onto the next thing.

Do I get everything I want? Not always. I can think of great delays and me pleading to no avail with spirit as to why I couldn't have what I wanted. I think I just exhausted them, and they gave in so I got it. AND BOY, DID I GET IT. These were not good, but little did I know at the time that those things came complete with LIFE LESSONS. BLEH!

If something doesn't happen, I have learned to pause and question if there is a reason. I'm not perfect. I *am* protected though. I don't always see it at the time and have thrown my fair share of temper tantrums. I have a visual of spirit going—OK, GO AHEAD! GIVE HER WHAT SHE WANTS—completely exasperated at my never-ending whining as to why I can't have what it is that I wanted. NOW? HA! I so know!

I happened to be on Amazon and found this really cool planter. It was similar to the chia pet-type vases. I put it in my cart to buy it but never hit the purchase button. It was a frivolous purchase at the time. It was so cool though! I kept looking at it; I was drawn to it in a big way. I just put it off to the side for something to get in the future. Lo and behold, drumroll please, I got it. HOW? you ask ... I traveled to my son's home over the holidays and out on their patio, on a shelf, is this exact planter complete with a thriving plant inside that complemented it. I lit up like a kid and told them I just saw that this past week and had the exact one in my cart on Amazon. They both asked, in unison, "Do you want it?" I was beside myself! How cool is it that the exact plant that I really wanted was suddenly being gifted to me! Did I manifest it? Or was spirit showing it to me? I do not care either way! I am so happy about this cute little plant and vase.

I am working on being more self-aware. I have semiretired my tornado-ish tendencies and have tried to be more in the moment and allow things to unravel.

I deliberately test, on occasion, and manifest a great parking spot, or such. I know now it is my runner/helper angels that are helping me. I don't rush. I pause to say THANK YOU.

There's been a sense of calm over me this year that I haven't had for a while. Mostly, it's there because there have been some very nice, positive things that have gone on. There are SO many more things that have personally blown me away. I know I was promised all of these positive things and was encouraged to get out of my head and just allow it to come when it's time. NOT RACE. I have been receiving them but not always when I expect to. I have been practicing being more present, truly just aware of where I'm at and not worrying about tomorrow, not thinking about yesterday, just being where I am.

Spirit's trip down memory lane and my manifestation skills have been insightful to say the least. I am a work in progress but forever and always grateful!

26

LIGHT ON THE HORIZON

I am an optimist at heart and yet there are times when I'm always looking for what could go wrong so that I am completely prepared. Call it a bad habit, but one that has served me well. I also have learned that this is a trauma response from years past. I still do it, though, at least until the hard stuff I may be going through is over. Not everything is rainbows, butterflies, and unicorns, yet. So, I try to stay one step ahead.

I have not had to put my dukes up in a while, though. There seems to have been a lightness and energy shift. Happiness is now steadier and more consistent. For the first time in a while. I consistently feel it!

That being said, I am completely aware of the many good things that have been showing up in my life. Many things have cleared up without much effort, if any, on my part. I am so aware and overly grateful! Spirit might say it is because I let things go. I think I was just so busy that I paid no attention to things and the energy just left.

The weeks have been insanely busy. I knew that they would be, and I don't mind. Frankly, it keeps me out of trouble. When I say trouble, I mean mentally I don't have any more brain cells left at the end of the day to overthink anything. I consider it a gift most days.

As I became more and more aware of how things are lining up, spirit reminded me of a recent message they gave me. I was so happy with the answers that I got! I know there's a lot of good stuff coming up for all the hard work that I've been putting in.

The message was that I am almost out from under some storm clouds and finally getting to someplace warm, sunny, and peaceful. I just remember I was going to make damn sure that I did everything in my power that nobody disrupts it.

The new riches in my life are now *peace*. I am super aware when the scales start to tip out of balance, so I get it back *in* balance. It feels amazing to finally be at this point so consistently. I'm truly grateful!

27

GOAL SETTING

Spirit nudged me to reflect on all the good things that have transpired in my life recently. Not everything happened all at once, but I believe spirit wanted me to look at the big picture to see and acknowledge how they truly have been helping me. Although some people would look at these things and take them for granted, I do not. When you have been through the fires of transformation, every single thing is amazing! It's like you start to breathe and live again. A huge shout-out to my angels and loved ones that helped me!

It started with me sitting down and writing my goals for the year. I asked myself what I wanted in this one year and what I wanted to accomplish. I wrote it all out. This was not what I *thought* I could do, it's what I wanted. I came up with a final number of what I needed to make for the year to pay off every single thing that I owed. This included vacations I wanted to take, services for self-care, car maintenance and repair, and money that I wanted to save. Seeing all this on paper is more of a road map for me. Personally, I break the numbers down to an hourly basis as this is more manageable than one lump sum figure.

When I am done with what I need to accomplish per hour, I have a counsel meeting with my spirit team. I basically read out everything on my list, what the main goal is and ask for their divine help in achieving it. Some might call this a prayer but honestly, I talk to them all the time as if they were in physical form in front of me. I also use the words OR BETTER in those prayers and statements. I am always surprised when my goals are surpassed because of this! My angels and spirit guides are delivering! No, they didn't show up at the door with a check but gave me the *opportunities* to make my goals manifest.

For example, they have placed ready, willing, and able clients who want to work with me in real estate. My business opportunities have grown thus helping me financially. They were all easy transactions, too. That's how I know without a doubt that it was a gift! When you work in real estate, there are some deals that are super easy and some that test every nerve and fiber of your being. Since what was presented to me was easy dealings, that was how I knew and felt that they were gifts.

Through work I made the money I needed to pay off bills and obligations. Just for the record, it is not the first time they have done this for me so I had the utmost faith they could do it again, and that they did!

Another goal was to secure my own place again while rent prices were skyrocketing. I got a nudge to drive through some neighborhoods I had not been through in a while. It took a while, but I found something that was not on the open market. It was a simple sign in the yard. The location was great, the manager was "old school" and, in my opinion, didn't have a clue what the market currently was. I can't put into words everything I have to say about finding this place. All I can exclaim is that this was a massive gift. This landlord was indeed an ANGEL put in my life path to help me at what spirit felt was the right time.

Furniture was on the goal list. I had a few new pieces in my storage pod that was still in North Carolina but not everything I needed. In my new place there was an air mattress, a camping chair, and one tray table. I verbally asked my angels in prayer, to help me find a couch. I honestly didn't know how I was going to get one in my budget let alone get it home. I also didn't have a trailer hitch for my car as it was in North Carolina with my other belongings to be shipped to me. I knew I would have to wait for the money to come in to buy something temporary. GUESS WHAT? I stopped over at a client's condo to return the air mattress they loaned me before I could buy my own. While visiting them, they mentioned that they were getting new furniture and asked me if I needed a couch and chair that they only had used seasonally? Of course, I jumped and said yes! They even offered to deliver it because their new stuff was coming the next morning. YOU CAN'T MAKE THIS STUFF UP! I was placed there at the right time, and I am insanely grateful for this. I checked this off my goal list as completed!

Extra money was earned so that I could finally pay to ship my pod of belongings back from North Carolina. I now had a place to ship them to, a place to put them, and help to unload them. GIFT, GIFT, GIFT.

In the meantime, though, Agent 007 had asked me what I still needed in the way of supplies for my new place. I gave her a list of things I felt I needed to get from the store. She called me the next day. She had a laundry basket full of a lot of what I needed. Everything was brand new, and she even had a lot in there I didn't think of. It actually took me two days to go through it all because of being so busy with work. Some might say it's the little things but, again, to me, they were HUGE.

Another client was moving, and asked if I needed spices or canned food as they didn't want to throw them away nor pay to ship home. Of course, I said, heck yeah! It was a lot of little miscellaneous stuff that I won't have to buy. Everything adds up! I checked this off the goal list as well.

My mom and her husband helped me in ways I cannot ever explain or make anyone comprehend. There is not enough space here to share how they helped me. Let's just say they were my biggest cheerleaders.

There were a lot of other people who helped in ways that they could. I could go on and on and mention them all. Absolutely nothing went unnoticed. I wrote and said many a thank-you. I am forever grateful.

I went into the post office to get my mail, again THANKING MY SPIRIT TEAM OF ANGELS that made me feel like I had won the lottery to be helped over and over again within weeks. I got in the car, and the radio was on, playing "THIS IS HOW WE DO IT" by

Montel Jordan. I literally just busted out laughing. Spirit puts their two cents in so I can get the message loud and clear.

Again, most of these situations and events would be minor to some people. I know it looked different to me when I was in a different place. Now, after experiencing a place of being stripped down, fresh out of the fire and barely bare-bones living, I take nothing for granted. I felt elated and fresh, full of gratitude.

Gratitude has always been a part of my vocabulary. I just wanted to put out there that seeing things from a different perspective has been one of the hardest things I have had to endure, but one that also has left a lasting impression on me. Things are continuing to look up. The goals for the year are indeed being checked off, one by one, with the help of spirit.

28

SEEING SIGNS FOR OTHERS

T he more aware you are of how this life supposedly works, the more tuned in you get. But I've had three unique instances in the past two weeks.

In my defense it's really stinking cool to not only have a front-row seat but also to see the astonishment on people's faces. Do I silently and sometimes go *na-na-booboo*? Yes. Do I want to exclaim with exuberance, "I told you so?" Hell, yeah! Do I? No. Why? Well, I respect that everyone's at a different part of their journey and it's not my job to convince anyone of anything. I am simply a helper right now.

Instance number one is that my friend was moving back to where she grew up. I keep telling her she could roll around in dog poop right now and come out smelling like a rose. Seriously, she has had so many things lined up for her so exquisitely, you would literally have to overlook the obvious not to see it. She's had a nudge and she's paid attention to it but on top of that her Auntie Rose, who passed away many years ago, has been showing up in *my* life to make sure that she gets the message: *SHE NEEDS TO MOVE.* For one, Auntie Rose identified herself at a mediumship meeting I had with a bunch of friends while in North Carolina. She also showed me Rose from *The Golden Girls* sitcom in a dream right before I woke up, which I thought was actually very clever! (I never watched it, but I am aware of the show and its characters.) Then, to boot, my friend was also getting messages a little here and a little there, but the icing on the cake was her putting some things away and a picture of Rose and my friend fell out of the picture frame face up. She was beside herself. Things have lined up so perfectly for her and I am so happy, but I told her that Auntie Rose has a magic wand and was certainly helping her on the other side! From the outside in, I saw the synchronicities of amazing events unfold and along the way, pointed out how these gifts of alignment were in her path because it was supposed to happen.

Another cool instance I witnessed was while standing with my friend in her mother's home who passed away a few months prior. We put the home on the market.

I had gone through and saged the house because the grief from her and her brother over her loss was energetically palpable to me. Clearing with sage and prayer gave it a fresh, clean feeling that was needed for the sale. I asked her mom through prayer to bless the house and bring forth a kind, willing and able person who may want to purchase it.

Lo and behold, they got an offer on this house. So, while I stood chatting with my girlfriend, she commented that her mom definitely must've had a hand in it. It was at this time that my Apple Watch went off and said the words out loud and in print *"**Right? It's how I work.**"* We could not stop laughing and we're so grateful for her assistance from the other side. I was able to snap a picture of it for proof before it turned off. We were in awe and yet grateful to get the message.

The third thing that happened was that we all received news that my father-in-law had passed away just hours before. I was at my son's babysitting my granddaughter and my son had just gotten home. I stayed a bit longer to make sure that he was doing OK. He said hi and took his gym bag to his bedroom to put it down.

I suddenly heard two knocks at the garage door like somebody wanted to come in. Not expecting anyone and my son in his room, I went to the garage door to see who was there. It was a profound knock! I opened the door and surprise, surprise, *there was nobody there*. OK, it could be a coincidence, right? I felt that it was a sign as I get knocks, pings and lights flickering a lot. Anyway, I was chatting with my son about a few things, and turned to look at my granddaughter. On the TV screen, frozen in place, was the word *"Grandad."* The cartoon *Bluey* was playing on the TV prior, but no one had touched anything, and it was just frozen on the screen. I pointed it out to my son (to subtly point out that I could not have orchestrated it) and said, "See, he's already sending us signs!" I'm pretty sure it was still on the TV when I left.

My son has not fully-fledged declared that he believes in signs but no doubt this was put in front of him to witness and help him to believe.

As I write this, I'm outside enjoying the breeze in thought about my father-in-law. There is an owl in the grass staring at me, inching its way closer to me. It has flown toward me twice and flown away. I asked if that was my father-in-law to please come back and show itself to me one more time. I am happy to report he's been back twice!

Each one of these instances has truly warmed my heart and I am so grateful to acknowledge the signs and show gratitude for them. Furthermore, I am grateful to witness the shock and awe on my various friends' faces. Although they may or may not believe in everything, it certainly plants a seed of wonder.

Our loved ones are truly on the other side helping to line things up and help us in any way that they can without interfering in our life path. It certainly brings a smile to my face to know this.

I mean seriously you can't make this stuff up!

29

PURGING AND MAKING SPACE

Note to self: *If it doesn't taste good going in, it's not going to taste good coming back up!*

Yep, I had food poisoning. I've never had it before and I never want it again! As I try to always see the silver lining in any situation, I was convinced I had purged myself down to a size 0. Not the case, but I felt I had a head start on a new diet.

I decided to lay low for a few days and regain my strength. I figured while I was sitting there, I might as well do something productive. I decided to start shredding and getting rid of documentation I was holding on to from ten years ago.

I'm pretty organized but as is with all businesses, there are some files I have to keep. Bleh!

I would like to personally give a shout-out to my cute little cross shredder. Although it could only handle six pages at a time and overheated quite a bit, it did the job. So, four movies and six large lawn leaf bags later (try saying that four times fast!), I had a massive head start in my quest to further purge.

When I truly looked at all that I needed shred, I asked myself why the hell was I not doing this when I was in lockdown from COVID for a year? Spirit popped in and said, *You weren't ready to let it go.* I had to ruminate on that statement for a bit.

I went through every file, but I am so glad that I did! There were pictures stuck in some files that I wanted to keep as well as many I was ready to throw away.

I was on a roll!

Next purge project: office supplies.

Being completely honest here, there should be a twelve-step program for my addiction to office supplies. I'm just saying.

Hello, my name is Lisa, and it has been four days since I got a new pad of paper, pens, and a stapler.

I allowed myself one letter-sized box to keep the supplies I wanted. Oh, it was hard for me to do but I did it! I felt like an office supply hoarder!

Seeing all the now-empty boxes piled on my patio fueled my desire to purge more!

I really sat with what spirit said about how I was *finally ready to let go.* What was different now?

Me.

I simply have reached a place where I am no longer interested in holding on to or maintaining anything that has zero relevance to my life. It wasn't just the physical part but the mental, emotional, and spiritual side I didn't realize was taking up space. I made note of this feeling. I finally understood what "letting go" meant. It is funny how spirit led me to this awareness.

The perfect trifecta of time, energy, and effort was there all because of food poisoning. A heaviness has lifted that I didn't realize that I was carrying.

If your hands are full and carrying the baggage of the old, you're not going to be able to fully receive the new.

I am so ready for the new stuff! Bring it, baby!

30

EGO MUCH OR ACKNOWLEDGMENT

Since starting this journey many years ago already, I have accomplished and learned a lot. I don't officially have a résumé though. I didn't realize how much I had done and accomplished until I was telling somebody I had never met before.

A good friend of mine has a coworker who has opened a woo-woo shop in the area. She made sure to give me their information, thinking it would be a good connection for each of us.

I went over to their new store and introduced myself. I felt very warm, inviting vibes. Being unsure of what my friend had explained about me, I wasn't sure what they knew of me or my capabilities.

As the conversation with the owners went on, spirit was channeling a plethora of ideas and inspirational nudges for them to cultivate. Of course, I have no idea if it was their vision, but the more I talked to them, I realized it was. I was grateful. The ideas were practically shooting out of my mouth to tell them.

As it happens at times when I channel, I feel I step outside myself and see what I am doing from an outsider's perspective. It is rather cool at times. This time kind of threw me though. I felt I was rattling off a woo-woo resume. This was a new one for me!

As to not come across as a newbie on the block, I rattle off different people I have studied with, the classes I've taught and taken, the groups that I have led, the podcast I did, and my participation in different events.

I want to stress that this list just popped into my mind and shot out of my mouth. I don't even have any of this written down! *What the hell?* I was outside myself watching all of this transpire as well as being inside myself looking out. I was seeing and hearing both perspectives at once.

I really do have a lot of things under my belt! I'm very grateful for every one of them. It's not like I picked up a book and now claim I am experienced, far from it. From the outside in, I was pretty damn impressed!

I've never put together a résumé about any of this. I never felt the need to. Like, if I sat down to do it right now, I don't think I would even remember half of what I said.

Then, I felt I was bragging. I started to question why I felt the need to speak about all these things. *Was* it bragging or necessary information? It truly was a very multisided thought that baffled me. I wasn't sure what to think about it.

After I got home, I thought about my interaction with these lovely people. I wondered if this was the resurrection of a long-standing habit of going overboard to prove my self-worth.

Why did I feel that I had to continue to share and give away all my ideas? Was rattling off an impromptu résumé really necessary? Did I not feel that I was good enough?

I think that's what it's boiled down to. I possibly felt the need to prove myself. I had to give to receive or be received. The recommendation of my friend should have been enough. Why did I feel the need to impress them further?

There's no question that spirit was using some of my experience to give them a foot up with ideas that could help them. They offered the use of their store if I want to do readings or do a class.

I'm still sitting on all this information. It could be a combination of everything; it could be a combination of nothing. I just was being a helpful person for the right reasons. My intentions were pure.

If this was about not feeling good enough, that needs to be addressed. So, I'm giving this more thought.

I am a fan of and have always operated out of the premise that my calling card would be word-of-mouth thus the reason I have no written resume. Spirit will lead the right people to me. This was definitely that connection.

I remind myself that everything happens exactly as it should. We were put in each other's paths for a distinct reason. We are here to help and heal. I just want to make sure that I address this for myself personally now and for my future.

31

MINI POP QUIZ! B+

I was due a commission for the closing of a file from my office. The comptroller questioned the wording on the closing statement for the party *we did not represent*. The state-controlled title company wrote the wording. To give herself leverage she decided to hold MY paycheck hostage until the issue was resolved. I knew hands down everything was done correctly. She felt *her interpretation* of how this wording should be was the correct way.

I felt I was being bullied into conforming. I stood my ground. I asked the manager to contribute their knowledge and back me up as they had been in the industry almost as long as I had. They also knew the ropes and the rules.

I want to stress that if my understanding of the rules and laws were incorrect, I would admit it. After thirty-plus years in the industry, I knew it was correct and the manager agreed.

So, guess what spirit decided to do? Give me a pop quiz!

Part A of the pop quiz was not to go into attack mode. I know, I know! Would it have been necessary to prove my point? No. Again, not only was this not my client but had nothing to do with our company.

Ah, this is when the channeling stuff kicks in now that I'm aware of it! Since the inquisition started via email, the reply that I *wanted* to send *kept getting scrambled, words kept getting messed up, erasures kept happening,* and I finally just wrote what came to me. (No doubt this was spirit's plan all along.) It was neither confrontational nor accusatory. Nor was it the *na-na-na-na boo-boo,* or what I really, really, really wanted to say!

I was very much aware that if, for some reason, something had changed that I was unaware of, I might have to stick my tail between my legs and it was better to stay neutral.

Lord, help me, I did not want to. I wanted to bow up and be in attack mode. I would be nice about it, but you would know without a doubt I was not a force to mess with if I started rattling cages. See, I'm *really good* at my job. I have had bumps and bruises and a thousand lessons over the years, and I know 1,000,000 percent that the paperwork that was done by a state-controlled third party was right. Yet they wanted to hold *my* paycheck back? *Tsk, tsk, tsk.*

The manager who had as much experience as me did her due diligence. After a few discussions we both felt everything across the board was correct.

Part B of this pop quiz was to let go and trust the manager to handle it. (*Dun dun DUUUUNNNNN!*)

Yeah, that didn't sit well with me. Trust me, *I trusted her.* I just wanted to get on the front lines of the fight. I had all my armor, my words, and experience in my corner. I was ready! Ready to go to battle and I had to sit back and let somebody *else* handle it.

I reluctantly agreed but it sat in my solar plexus and festered. A LOT. Of course, I am having this mental fight with nobody else but myself.

Members of the jury! Here is my plea about the client we don't represent and backup evidence! As you can see, it's an open-and-shut case!

So as my system on the outside looked very calm, it was what was going on *inside* that was in turmoil. On top of it all, it was also Friday late afternoon, which meant this was going to roll over until the next business day.

I was struggling with dealing with my emotions. I was ready to attack and could do *nothing* about it. There was nothing I could do because it wasn't a business day and there was no amount of jumping up and down hooting and hollering that I could do to change anything. My feelings, thoughts, and so on were mine to deal with all by myself. I couldn't even vent to a friend. There was nothing I could have said to any of my friends that would've made sense to them because they're not in the business. My passion, drive, and being a stickler for the details and rules in this case would have fallen on deaf ears.

On top of that, I had no more wine! Grocery shopping was on Saturday morning, and I had nothing that could make my brain just slow the hell down from running scenario after scenario. I was in a tornado of thoughts and feelings that I couldn't see my way out of or put a Band-Aid on. Trust me, this is new territory for me. I even caught my lessons-learned higher self-saying back to me, *sit with it. Deal with this now, alone. How and why are you feeling like this? Why don't you trust that it will be taken care of?* I ended up falling asleep distracting myself with an evening of TikTok videos.

At half past five in the morning, the first thing I wake up and start thinking about is the situation *all over again*. Except now I'm rested, recharged, and ready to wrestle this conversation again!

I made myself get out of the house. I felt like I had to go someplace, be someplace else, or I had to deal with somebody else other than my thoughts. So, I went to a new grocery store.

When I was done, I had one more errand to run and when it was complete, I took my ass to the park.

My higher self felt like the parent of my inner five-year-old having a temper tantrum. I had to go sit in the park, put my bare feet on the ground, and not move until my attitude changed!

I took my shoes off, took my camping chair out of the back of my car and placed it in the shade and sat my behind down. No phone canoodling. No singing, no music, no communication with anybody. I felt this unspoken command to just sit there. I was staring at the water and had trees all around me. This was a way better view than sticking my nose in a corner but the same in theory.

There were a couple times I looked at my feet, thinking there should be ants or some creepy-crawly and there was nothing.

FOUR HOURS WENT BY!

Yes, I'm ashamed to say it took me *four hours* before I was significantly aware that I felt different. I knew that I had been grounding and transmuting all the negative energy, frustration, anger, and so on into the earth. *Four freaking hours*! I wasn't even aware that much time had passed! It was like seeing the turkey button pop up to say, *OK you're done*, you're recharged, you may go now.

I got up and I felt relaxed, I felt calm, *I felt at peace.* Trust me, this was a far cry from what was going on in my head just hours earlier. I had released the angst and let it go. What was meant to be was going to be. Yes, *I was right.* But it was just a feeling of an inner knowing that everything was being taken care of all for my highest and best. It was also in that moment that I was really grateful that I had not ripped anyone a new one on paper. After all was said and done, I still needed to work with this comptroller. To quote my mother, *"Never put anything in writing that you wouldn't want to come back to you."*

I packed up my chair and left the park. I felt as if I had gotten a two-hour massage. It was that lazy, *wow this is really nice* feeling after you deeply relax.

My Saturday and Sunday were great! I got lots of other things done and I didn't worry my pretty little head off about *anything.*

On Monday morning, I knew that there was going to be more said, but I was confident I didn't have to dig my heels in or say anything derogatory.

I really had a few choice words to express and made a conscious decision to not say anything unsavory to prove a point. Guess what? The manager and I were indeed right that the state-run title company's wording was correct. Not only did what was being contested have nothing to do with our company or my compliance with any law but the way it was constructed was correct and validated by the legal counsel for the state.

I haven't been back in the office to see one of these particular people who was making the initial waves. I've sat back today and realized that it was a gift to be able to just go sit with my feet on the ground and regroup. Trust me, I rarely have issues that make needing to give myself a time-out a habit. I was really grateful to have the time and inner knowing to go sit in the park though.

I want to stress that my angels were in full force during all of this. I saw a lot of numeric signs like 1111, 1125, and 111, which were all significant messages for me. It was as if they were telling me, *Girl, go chill out! We got you!* Could I see and feel it at the moment? Not at all. There is a saying I heard recently: *You cannot see your reflection in boiling water. When the waters calm, clarity comes.*

I am not perfect, but I know my job and my ego blew up in defense of my experience in knowing many things in the industry. Boundaries were in full force to not take responsibility for a company that is governed by the state and not tolerate MY paycheck being held back.

The truth prevailed. It was a clear reminder to be aware of what you say, speak your truth, and stand in your power. Unlike the fiasco at Christmas, I remained calm. I responded and didn't react. Well, I reacted inside enough to know I had to let it go.

The only reason I didn't give myself an A+ in this pop quiz was because I had to give myself a time-out to get a hold of my emotions.

I am aware that was the preferred coping mechanism. I didn't have a glass of wine, go jogging or eat five pounds of cake. Baby steps.

So far, my pop quiz grades are an F and a B, giving my average a C-. I am making headway!

Dear Reader,

Grounding is essential in many ways. Having shoes on all the time disconnects you from the earth. Take them off and just stand on the dirt or ground. Many studies show the benefits of this. Every bit helps! I also bring up and share these pop quizzes as something to learn by. Step back and look at what you needed to learn from them. There is a reason for everything.

32

REVVING THE ENGINE

In the past few months, I feel the planetary alignments actually affected me. Something feels wonky.

I have never been so grateful to have a little cave of my very own to hide in for a short period of time while the world adjusts. The climactic events of governmental institutions have wreaked havoc on the whole world. Many around me have been feeling off energetically as well. We all just want to go hide for a bit!

Suddenly though, there's a lightness in my spirit. I feel like I'm revving the engine and getting ready to move forward again. It's felt like in the past few months everything has been put on pause. As much as I wanted to move forward, I have been told through meditations to just be still. Of course, I never stop addressing my never-ending to-do list. Hey, it keeps me out of trouble. I am happy to report that I am making great headway too.

Subtle things are happening though. I always have one eye open and pay attention to what's going on around me. Although there is not one instance that stands out profoundly among the others, I just feel it would be interesting to address these as I am more consciously aware.

1. I am starting to see repeating numbers in bulk. I always see them, but for a short duration it felt like there had been a pause. When my spirit team kicks it into higher gear and starts showing me the same number over and over again, it's a sign for me to start paying extra close attention. It means that something is about to happen. So right now, as the people on *Sesame Street* would say, today's numbers are 222, 555, 1010, and 1212. You see, I assigned a meaning to each one of these multiple numbers, which is my personal "sign language" with my angels. When I am out and about and see these numbers, translated they are a message to me. This set translated meant that spiritual upgrades are coming and to pay attention when they show up. These upgrades will result in changes and just go with the flow.

2. For the past few years now, I have been working on fixing things from the inside out. This means addressing and paying attention to my roots and foundation and doing inner work. In doing so, I haven't really cared about my outside appearance much. This has been quite freeing I might add. Although always presentable, I have decided to put working on the outside more on the front burner. This may or may not involve being more social and being more out and about. I honestly think I can attribute this sudden interest in putting in the effort to my friend Canada who has met someone that has done the work! I am feeling more hopeful for my personal future.

Mind you, I have friends and go places. I'm just not letting anything about me stand out (that I am aware of) to draw attention to myself. I reckon this is to my inner five-year-old wearing sunglasses and then thinking nobody can see them.

3. My dreams have increased tenfold! See, I pay attention to my dreams because a lot of them are prophetic in nature. I'm very much aware that this is a gift to know and receive this information. I am waking up with story after story.

When it comes to my dreams, which are often prophetic in nature, if I vocalize the correct interpretation, spirit will not repeat the dream. I think I've gotten pretty good at this deciphering stuff too! After having enough instances to look back on and reviewing the dreams I have recorded, I can see how spirit has presented the information to me, how I look at it, and what actually happened.

For example, I had a dream I lost my purse and the next night, I dreamt about a completely different situation, but again lost my purse. When I sat down and acknowledged what it means to me and how it looks, I stopped having the dream. Regardless, I pay attention to them suckers! They are pretty accurate! I highly recommend recording your dreams. It's pretty cool when you see and know about things ahead of time. Spirit has even tattled on people around me. Yep, I am in the know. I won't tell YOU what I know, but there is a lot I am aware of for sure!

4. Spirit has cleared the bench when it comes to my work. Oddly, though I'm not really worried. You see, spirit gave me this amazing gift of business to get me back on my feet financially. I had

the easiest jobs come to me, one right after the other. They were and have been amazing, simple, and relatively fun transactions.

Suddenly, there's nothing. Nada. All I hear are crickets in my real estate business world! This never lasts forever so I don't panic. I just have this nudge that this gift of time is meant for me to get my to-do list chiseled down, my affairs in order, and take care of other things that need to be addressed. Instead of worrying about it I just feel like it's a gift of time for me to utilize. Working ahead on things brings me great joy sometimes.

5. My readings for others ebb and flow. Being busier than other times, spirit is very much aware that when my energy is not on point, not to bring people to me for readings. For this I am truly grateful. Spirit puts people in my path to help. So, if I'm spread really thin, they're not going to lead or nudge people to contact me. I would be doing a disservice to them and to spirit. When the readings start picking up, it's an *atta-girl* that my energy is on point, and I am to help.

6. It almost feels like there's been an intermission between life chapters. I don't know how to explain it, really. Like my life is a play or movie and this is the intermission. New players, people, and circumstances are all moving into position for the next chapters. There's a lot of shuffling going on right now! I have stepped back and looked at everything from a broader perspective. I think I can see the potential of channeled readings and future events that are going to align. I don't have all the details just yet. I have to wait like everybody else.

So, you see, there's a lot of little things that seem to be clues to the bigger picture shifting and changing. In the past, I would have just not paid attention to any of this and just did what I normally would have done. Now, though, I'm taking advantage of the downtime to reset, recoup, realign, and keep going. I am not looking a gift horse in the mouth at all! I'm trying to practice not sweating the small stuff.

A friend called to tell me she found a literal puzzle piece on the grass while out for a walk. We joked that this was a sign and a small piece in the bigger picture of things to come. At least we have a head start. In the meantime, I will rev my engine, so I am ready when the next part starts!

33

VERBAL PUSH-BACK AND BOUNDARIES

I recently had a friend who pretty much ripped my head off for offering a potential solution to a problem she repeatedly complained about. It was just a suggestion. Did she ask for my help? No.

My bad!

She honestly didn't think she said or did anything wrong. How she talked and what she normally said were pretty much the same. To her it was *normal.* After this happened there were parting salutations and we hung up. After, I was in a whirlwind of emotions! I was MAD! Mad at myself!

First and foremost, I let someone talk to me the way she did. None of my other friends have *ever* spoken to me like that and yet I allowed it. Friendship or not, that was a hard boundary I had established that I obviously didn't adhere to. I didn't speak up and use my voice. I was extremely frustrated by what she said to me but way more irritated at myself! Seriously, what good are boundaries if I didn't enforce them? I had zero intention of talking to her ever again except when absolutely necessary.

Spirit wouldn't let this issue rest. Oh, I smelled a spiritual lesson in all of this!

First of all, I tried to see where she was coming from. She was so immersed in her problem she couldn't fathom the solution I offered. The repetitiveness with which she spoke of this issue made me think that she didn't really *want* help. If the solution wasn't exactly how she wanted, it was not an option. I have been in this place more times than I care to admit. So, I get it.

I was still angry with myself.

Funny thing was, she didn't see anything wrong with her actions and called me back a few days later to chat again *as if nothing happened*. Oh, but guess what? She mentioned having a fallout with a *different* mutual friend. (HA! *Imagine that!*)

After her complaining about that person, she mentioned that *if there was ever something that I wanted to get off my chest, or if I had a problem with something she's done or said, to please bring it up.* No question this was a moment I was not going to pass up to speak my mind. I had nothing to lose!

I did not skip a beat and dove right in. I didn't think twice about bringing this up. It was one of those moments where I can look back and say, "Oh my goodness, spirit is channeling through me." This is where I got to voice my concern and get it off my chest. (Hey, she asked!) I'll be damned if I was going to sweep this one under the rug.

I know now that spirit uses my voice and choice of words like a puppet at times to get a point across to people. I channel things in such a manner that, if nothing else, they plant a seed. There was no question that spirit was involved in her calling me again. This was definitely one of those times.

I reminded her of the last time we talked, what she talked about, how she acted and what she said to me. I then told her what a great mood I was in prior to her call and her effect on me after.

Then, I owned my part in our conversation. I **_apologized_** to her and told her she was indeed right! She did NOT ask me to fix her or her problem. I told her that I have a habit of wanting to take on other people's lives and fix them, but I was truly sorry for trying to help when not asked.

Of course, *then* I flipped the script. Without skipping a beat or any hesitation, I told her that the way she treated me would **NEVER** happen again. I reminded her that I was not her personal dumping ground. Just because I picked up the phone to chat didn't give her an open invitation to word vomit shit all over my life. I was under zero obligation to stop what I was doing, no matter what mood I'm in, and listen. (And this was the best part!) The new rule is: *If I have to ask permission to help you fix your life or just listen,* **you** *have to ask permission to vent to me!*

I made it clear to her that I am out of the weeds, and I have zero obligation to **_anyone_** to climb back in. I will do everything in my power to protect the peace and the solitude that I have finally done the work to get back. If that means losing a friendship because I won't be somebody's dumping ground or verbal punching bag, then so be it! At this point in my life, I have no problem striking the match and burning the bridge!

After my very stern retaliation, her mood changed, and we had a conversation about this issue. She did admit that if I had approached her with this issue at the time of the prior conversation, she would've gone off the deep end. She was not ready to hear it. Looking back at the timing made sense because I honestly wasn't ready to discuss it with her. I had to see where my part was in all this. But since she brought it up, the floodgates opened, and I held nothing back. I felt better.

This was no doubt a teaching moment for each of us.

If you play games on your phone like I do, there are some days you just continue to repeat the same level over and over again. You keep doing what you've been doing, thus getting what you've been getting. Some levels last, what seems, forever. Then, one day, you play and suddenly, the moves work and you are off to the next level. Ta-da! It is not that you understand exactly what you did but just the smallest tweak made the difference. This really is like life in general. Some levels you are stuck in and others you fly through. I told my friend this and she said, "Wow, that's a really good example."

I have learned so much and I am practicing what I have learned. Guess what? It works! If I'm stuck it's usually not for very long. I swear life is almost like the game of *Jumanji*. You don't know what's going to come next, but you're stuck until you have the tools to get out.

Anyway, the conversation with my friend ended with a lot of gratitude and appreciation on both our parts. Not all friends will just point-blank tell you that you really irritated them or agree to discuss it and fix it. I used to be one of them. I would sweep it under the rug, letting you say whatever you wanted without ever speaking up. But oh, baby, not anymore!

There is no handbook to life. We can't cheat and look at the table of contents or the index in the back. We have to go through each chapter. Sometimes we're stuck on a chapter because we don't understand until suddenly, we do.

34

JUMPING TO CONCLUSIONS

I am a recovering rule maker. Call it a childhood protection method. If I make rules, then I can adapt. I have made many declarations because of this. *THIS is the way it will always be!* If I had a crappy day, I would make a rule about it. If there was a twist or turn and I felt like this was going to be the new norm, it was my way of adjusting and making it easy for me going forward. I now know that this is a trauma response from living with volatile people in my life.

In some ways, I think my pessimistic side has helped. If I thought of all the things that could go wrong and adjust accordingly and prepare, it would be less traumatic for me. Yup! That was me! I had a backup plan for the backup plan. *ALWAYS PREPARED.* There were no emotions about anything, I did what I had to do. I needed to assure my inner child we would be safe.

Ask me if that's working anymore?

N-O-P-E.

There have been so many twists in my life that I can no longer make ANY rules. Just when I would make the rule I would wait five minutes, and things would change. Has this been easy to adjust to? Not-at-all. Spirit has stripped me of my almighty security blanket! My protection mode. They want me to rely on *THEM*. My faith. Use my gifts, to WAIT, let go, and allow. To know that I am safe no matter what.

I had to do a lot of shadow work to heal my inner child. I will protect her now and forever. Lately I have had to convince both of us we'll be safe without making a rule or preparing for the worst. I have learned through all of this that I cannot even jump to conclusions. I have had to practice waiting and watching and tapping into my higher self to see how it unfolds.

As much as I am allergic to patience, spirit has been kind to me in this lesson. It has been a slow process for me to let this tried-and-true habit go even after I did the shadow work. I knew what the reasons were, where it came from, and how I needed to overcome it. It didn't mean I threw this security blanket in the trash. I folded it nicely and put it on a shelf to pull down anytime I might need it.

What I have learned is that just because there is a change or a shift, I do NOT know everything about the situation or all the participants. I cannot jump to conclusions at all and write a story I don't know anything about.

Spirit gently reminds me that I need to pause and wait for the remaining pieces to work themselves into the appropriate position. Ten times out of ten, it's not what I was thinking. I would have jumped to a conclusion and made a rule, and it would have been wrong.

I know I've said it before, and I'll say it again, that I am a work in progress. I am getting better. I can honestly say I've come a long way with all of this, but I still have my moments. Even with my intuition, channeling and dreams, there is no cheat sheet or shortcut for me or my life experiences. Furthermore, they don't happen when I snap my fingers either.

So now that I am fully aware that new chapters of my life starting, spirit has been doing a lot of shifting of circumstances in and out of position. People you think are going to be around have moved or changed areas. Situations that seem consistent, reliable, and repetitive are now different and evolving. Again, spirit has told me to just pause, wait and look around. Circumstances don't involve me but could affect me.

That they have.

Honestly, old habits die hard. Yes, I have bitten my tongue about creating a rule recently, which is why I am bringing this up. Spirit said, *What was once one way will be another shortly.* I am now keenly aware of how much I have been holding my breath to see if anything else was shifting. Spirit does not let me work ahead. I am to be patient and watch and wait. I am safe. I am protected. I no longer have to put up my defenses. Now I know.

I have to admit that some of this has been fascinating. It's a new thought process to handle life this way. It is working too!

I am sure I have been kept on straight and narrow paths because I have not changed courses midstream, jumped to conclusions and created a rule to adapt. Spirit isn't even allowing me in the pool area to hold my nose and jump two feet in. Now that I am listening, I hear or get the nudge to pause, watch, and see. I'm really glad that I have had to wait because the rules I would have made would not have benefited anybody. Quite a few times, I've actually saved face. Yes, that was my ego speaking. Dear ego, *go sit down.*

I am going to go out on a limb here and say that I'm sure there are going to be many more changes coming. What's fascinating is that now that I'm aware of what's to come, it's more of an invitation, in general terms, to sit back and watch the process from the big picture.

Spirit told me the only thing they wanted me to do was jump rope, not jump to conclusions. I just know that sometimes when I'm reading a book, I speed read. Even when I listen to audiobooks, I listen to them at 1.5x speed because a lot of people just move and speak too slowly for me. It is a habit to do things fast.

In the big picture again, allowing is receiving—and the divine feminine, and going fast is DOING—which is the divine masculine. I am still working on this. I'm giving myself an atta-girl. I feel like this was a little bit of a pop quiz for me to see how I would handle a lot of moving parts suddenly shifting. In my mind, it's kind of like looking at the intricacies of the gears of a grandfather clock. On the front, it looks simple but inside there are many gears that move and shift at appropriate moments to create the next movement of the hands of time.

Let's hope this keeps going!

35

HIGH-LOW GAME

It had been a hot minute since I left the house, so my soul said, *Take me out!* I obviously needed a change of scenery for the day. My soul was insistent and very persistent! Mind you, I am only working on about three hours of sleep right now, but something woke me up and I just wanted to get going! I had everything ready including my list of things to do. So, I jumped in the car and got going.

My list included running errands, grabbing some breakfast, and park time for some grounding. See? I knew spirit had a reason for me to get up early and go!

The river water at the park was like glass. I could not help but hope that the person I was manifesting to come into my life would have a boat. Being out on a boat sounded so inviting to me. To boot, there were two boats cranking some really good rock music that echoed across the water toward me. I am hooked on a boat and good tunes at sunrise any day of the week.

I got up to throw some trash away and came across a feather. I love these kinds of signs. My day was off to a great start!

Next on my list was a stop at my office to print off paperwork I had been stockpiling. This included all the dreams I have been talking into my phone that have time and date stamps. Also, the translation of all the channeled messages for myself tends to create a hefty pile every so often to keep my notebook up to date. There were so many significant messages gifted to me that I want to keep them all in one place.

Let me tell you, I was over-the-top elated to get all of this done in one day! Going to the water and grounding, plus getting up and out early really put a pep in my step for the day!

As I was printing things off, one transcribed reading caught my eye, and I ended up reading it before I printed it. I was aware of the swirl of emotions I felt just reading it again. Mind you, these words came from spirit through me, and I still felt a lot of emotions just rereading it. I don't feel the emotions when I channel for myself 99 percent of the time. This gal is simply the microphone.

This was weird, though! The message was like a roller coaster. *Great things are coming! There are rewards for all the work I have done.* One part was a bunch of declarations of rainbows, butterflies, and unicorns to come.

But WAIT! There was more!

Then there were warning statements of things I cannot control. *You will feel out of sorts and not know where to turn. Some will make you feel attacked.*

Can we say BUZZKILL?

It's like a freaking roller coaster!

Let me tell you about me and roller coasters. *I LOVE THEM.* Well, I used to, but now, not so much. I still go on them. My body doesn't care for them as much as my inner child did. So, I hold my breath. In some subconscious way, I tell myself that if I just hold my breath for three minutes and twenty-eight seconds more, the ride will be over. I know I can do it! It is uncomfortable but I manage.

As fast as the ride starts it's over and I can exhale. Yes, I will smile and talk about how great it was and my insides are going, *OH, HELL NO!*

Sometimes reading what I channel is like a roller coaster ride. It is full of really high highs, super-low dips, a few sharp turns and every so often a loop-de-loop. Since reading is just a proverbial roller coaster you would think I would handle it better. Eh, not so much!

There have been many channeled readings that point-blank state, "*Do not embellish what we are telling you. It's not as bad as you think. The hard stuff is over.*"

Well, some parts of certain readings sound pretty damn scary the way they were worded. I can't hold my breath forever.

Eventually whatever is going to take place *will* be over, but everybody has to play their part. No one is going to hurry on account of me just because I am holding my breath. So here I am wanting to get it done, get it over with.

While I have psyched myself up for it, I want to clap my hands and yell, **let's go, let's go, let's go!** so I can get on to the good stuff. Unfortunately, the more I put my radar up to try to figure out what's going on, the more it's kept away from me.

Spirit knows I do this. To make sure I get the full-bodied effect, they wait until I am not looking, then blindside me. Sometimes, it feels like this is a cruel joke spirit plays on me. I know there's a reason. Once I am out of it and look back, I can see the big picture but during, it stinks sometimes.

I have been warned that I have done everything that I need to do except one thing. There is one more big thing coming up and a "roller coaster of emotion" has been used to describe it. I have been assured though that along with the ups that will be really high highs, there will be really low lows.

You know, I don't know if there's enough Botox in this world to keep the stress lines off of my face at this point. It's taken me a good few years to grow back all the hair I lost from stress. So, to hear that there's one more big thing? UGH! It has also taken me a good long time to get in touch with my emotions. Like, couldn't we have done this when I was stoic and unfeeling? To boot, I know that whatever "THIS" thing is will NOT be done fast enough for me to hold my breath. Nope, not a three-minute thirty-eight-second fix. It's a little unnerving to say the least!

Although I can feel that it's coming up soon, I have learned over the years that very rarely, if ever, does it happen when I think it will.

Telling close friends what spirit has revealed to me is never in my timeline though.

CHECK, PLEASE!

I have stopped and wondered what's the point of knowing if you aren't going to be able to control it? Of course, the flip side of all this is that if they wanted me to control it, I would be told. Which they aren't, so I can't.

Oh, and you know that old saying, "The only way out is through?" Spirit also states they want me to have more experiences that will result in more stories to tell.

Despite what I think are delays, I've made a lot of forward movement. I am really waiting for "And she lived happily ever after, THE END." PLAY OVER!

These channeled messages speak of specific names, windows of time, circumstances, and players mentioned. I just honestly don't know what year. I can't hold my breath that long. I can barely make it across the pool sometimes!

In one of the channeled messages, it said that I need to go through and make notes, which I'm going to do. Spirit doesn't hand you all the answers, they give you the advice you need so you can make as much of an educated decision as possible. I'm just not always good at taking advice, even from spirit.

I guess we shall see! Maybe I will just put a parachute on for the high highs and my scuba gear on so I can breathe in the deep end.

The gift of time and extra motivation to get all these other projects done distracts me and I am grateful.

They want my plate clean and my hands empty. So, for now, I will keep up with my to-do list and stay busy avoiding any roller coaster in the process.

36

MY GPA IS RISING!

I passed an open-book test. It was a very close call though!

First of all, I think it's interesting how similar most of the players in your life are when you actually start looking at it. Granted, not everybody is exactly the same, but most of them are. They are just wrapped in different packages. That is why you're told during this awakening and healing process that if you don't fix it, you're going to keep getting lessons to learn over and over again, just with different people.

THIS IS SOOOOOO true!

This open-book test started from a text message I received from someone in my past. If there was a camera on me as I read it, I turned into a human flame from the ground up. Just so you know, I still have horns!

Yes, I know I channel angel messages, but you cannot have the light without the dark. Well, my dark side puffed its chest up, smeared camouflage paint under my eyes and wanted to go to war.

My initial response was to pick up the phone and retaliate back. Although what they said to me was relatively polite, it crossed a boundary *I NEVER SET*. This person has crossed unspoken boundaries many times before and continues to try. My bad for not nipping this in the bud when I should have.

GAME ON!

I immediately picked up my phone to retaliate but then put the phone down. I would pick it up again, start texting, put the phone down. After a solid five minutes of my brain turning into a full-blown circus act of tricks and comments, I called Agent 007 and asked her to infuse some sanity into me.

I was surprised she did not take my side! Like, I just knew I was in the right 1,000,000 percent. I absolutely knew I was right and could say so with my newfound boundaries in place. I wanted to exercise them.

Agent 007 simply said that because I never spoke up there was implied consent on my part. Therefore, there had to be a compromise.

Seriously? UGH! I was pretty shocked, but I listened to her reasoning.

The issue was that *over a year ago*, somebody made the decision to throw a party, make purchases all by themselves, and then handed me a bill for half the cost. They never even told me about this, consulted with me, asked for my opinion, or questioned if I was ABLE or wanted to help. Nope, they threw a party, spent money, took the credit and handed me a *handwritten* bill.

Mind you, I was just a guest at this party. I was no different than anyone else. I was not given credit or acknowledgment for being a cohost. I was not granted access to any information about anything but was just told a date and time. So, two days later, it shocked the knickers off me when I heard I was responsible for half of the bill!

Did I say something then? NO. So that was my mistake. A boundary was crossed, and I didn't speak up or say anything. I literally had just moved back into town and was living out of a suitcase. I'd been there for maybe a week at best.

Given the circumstances of the person the party was being thrown for, I didn't mind helping or contributing. I was never asked, though. They just assumed they had full access to my bank account for whatever they felt was "reasonable." The receipt for all they spent was handwritten and even added up incorrectly, despite them saying they didn't want to "nickel and dime" me. I saw and signed no contracts, had no say on what vendors would be used, or any details. Just the bill two days AFTER the party.

Financially, I was not able to contribute at the time. I never said anything other than I would get money to them when I could. Yep, another mistake.

So, time went on and, honestly, we had both forgotten the obligation. Or so I thought. Now, a year and a half later, I get the text message stating that I had "long enough," and I needed to pay up my portion of the money for this party.

A year and a half later, I have regained my power. My strength. My resolve. My sanity. My sleep. My life. My backbone.

LET'S GET READY TO RUMBLE!

Now, I've got lots of things to say! Like, so much so that I feel like my higher self looked at me and said, "What are you doing and who the hell are you?"

So, when Agent 007 mentioned that maybe a reduction in the payment would be the correct response versus not paying it at all, well, that pretty much floored me. Talk about taking the wind out of my sails!

I made myself sit with it. I had to let it roll around in my brain, step away from it for a while, and then look at it differently. The old version of myself was fired up and ready to really let them have it. The new and improved version of me had its own reply and a few choice words to go along with it. Obviously, me, myself and I could not agree.

The biggest question that spirit brought to my attention was, *Why was I so ready to fight?* Why was I so mad? Why did I feel the need to blow up and not respond but react? Oh, it's the bane of my existence sometimes. That's what I am supposed to do: set boundaries and use my words. SPEAK UP!

Honestly, I was feeling ganged up on. No one was taking my side. What the hell!

You see, being a recovering people pleaser, I've always taken the stance in the past of just playing nice. Then I would hope and pray that the other people would do the same. But it turned out that I was being taken advantage of. Well not anymore. There's a new sheriff in town.

Back to the issue that was circling the drain. Why was there so much anger to try to hurt this person back with words and nonpayment?

After a few hours, spirit finally illuminated to me the reason for my anger. Did I feel justified? YEP! I finally had a small way to poke back after them poking me for many, many years, and now I wasn't allowed to! Spirit told me to come up with a different plan of action.

I didn't overstep my bounds with this person. I know there are some feelings from the past on their side as well. They have tried for years to poke me where they think it will hurt. I have shown nothing nor ever given them that satisfaction. *Hurt people hurt people.* They were trying to hurt me again and here I was trying to hurt them back. I am only responsible for myself. The anger that I had no idea had built up was there and I had to address it.

On top of all that, this person has also been in my dreams a lot prior to this text message. Between channeled messages I received and my dreams, I am privy to things going on in their life. It's not pretty. It also made sense why they were now, finally, asking for the money.

None of that stopped me from pulling out the big guns of my righteous attitude.

Agent 007 encouraged me to show some grace because of the circumstances in this person's life. I wanted to use the circumstances of what I knew to my advantage, but I didn't. It wouldn't be right. It's not who I am or what I represent. I had fault in this as well.

What I lacked was the right words to say that would allow me to get my point across without being overly wordy or throwing stronger jabs. You know: state the facts, give back what I got and take a stand. I really wanted to get it all off my chest. But I didn't. They got the G-rated version. I kept my bag of tricks handy, ready to strike if necessary. Agent 007 gave me a few words that I felt I could utilize. I agreed to communicate in a different fashion at a different time, taking the high road.

Quite a few hours had passed since I received the initial text message. It took me *that long* to see things differently. I had finally calmed down—enough. I returned a text simply telling them what I would agree to contribute, which was not what they demanded of me, and hit send.

They must've been sitting on their phone watching and waiting. Their response back implied that they were frustrated and angry. I could tell that they didn't have the energy to dig into this, so they reluctantly conceded with what I was going to contribute.

When I read their reply, I reminded myself that just because they were angry doesn't mean they were right! Their anger has nothing to do with me.

Agent 007 was very proud of me and said I did the right thing. I know I did, but I still wanted to lash out. I'm going to need to sit with this for a little bit because I think there is more to it.

True to their fashion, they did not listen to nor want to hear my side. This is one of the reasons we no longer talk. Again, there's a difference between listening to understand and listening to defend.

They were truly in a listening-to-defend frame of mind. So was I, for a bit.

Despite the mental gymnastics going on behind the scenes, I did come across cool, collected, and direct thanks to Agent 007. I was feeling like a cross between Elle Woods from *Legally Blonde* and Johnny Depp's attorney.

I know this person very, very, well. I have a feeling that there may be further retaliation and verbal comments as our paths will cross in the future. I have my bag of things to say if necessary. As of now, I have drawn a line in the sand. I finally set the boundary. They are someone who will complain about me whether I do something good or bad. They are firmly seated in victim mode and have everyone around them fooled that nothing is their fault. Spirit is taking care of them now, though. Funny, I never saw them this way up until now.

Even the muddiest of waters will clear once left alone. I hope someday they see things differently.

As for the pop quiz, I had to use the open-book option and lean on Agent 007 for rationality. True to form, she came through.

I am glad that I backed away until I saw the bigger picture in it all. Again, it's not what I wanted to do but they are hurting enough right now. I didn't need to turn the knife.

The open-book test grade has bumped my GPA average up! It was a close call!

37

WHERE THE HELL DID I GO?

Astral travel is an intentional out-of-body experience (OBE). Your soul or consciousness is often called an "astral body." It is separate from the physical body and capable of traveling outside it throughout the universe. So, have you been anyplace lately?

When Agent 007 and I purchased Apple Watches it was to be more hands-free and break away from always having to be by my phone. I want more human contact. We felt very high-tech to say the least.

I discovered an app that tracks sleep on my watch. This was going to be interesting! Why? I DREAM ALL-THE-TIME. This app also tracks your heart rate. I could see when I got up to use the bathroom and see the long stretches of sleep and when I tossed and turned.

In learning about all things woo-woo, the discussion and information of astral travel has come up. I tucked it away in my memory bank. It could explain some of my dreams that feel so real! Seriously, my dreams feel *so* real sometimes that I don't even remember that I live a completely different life when awake.

Ever have one of those dreams where you feel yourself wake up and go through your normal morning routine? Yep, you have your coffee, get in your car to go to work, hear a horn blaring and realize it is your ALARM? You then discover you haven't even gotten out of bed yet! WEIRD, isn't it? *It felt so real!* That is an example of this.

Since I dream a lot, this app on my watch might give me a way to analyze my dreaming state and also how much I tossed and turned for the night.

Luckily, I don't have to get up to use the bathroom more than once a night, if that. When I do, those are the hash marks in red. I have seen those since the get-go. So, TRUST ME when I saw super long stretches of red, my logical brain was trying to figure out WHAT THE HELL WAS THAT? What happened? The way I understood them was that I got up, which I hadn't. This happened two different nights. I can attest, I did not do anything *but* sleep. I remembered dreams upon waking both times as well. Same routine as always.

If I get any messages from my dreams, I write them down. Trust me, I was surprised looking at the app on these mornings. I noticed my heart rate and how the dots show it going down, disappear for a bit and then show back up and increase. Did I flatline? Sleepwalk? No clue. So, with the information on astral travel emerging around me, it makes me wonder if, for a short while, my soul left my body to go *somewhere*. Then, upon returning, it picked back up and moved into another dream. This has only happened twice, so I have ruled out a sleeping disorder. If that were the case, I would think it would happen with more frequency or in some sort of pattern. To date, these are the only two times it has happened.

One of these notifications stated that I was doing something from 1:55 a.m. to 3:30 a.m. That's a long time and no doubt I would have remembered if I was awake.

To add further intrigue, should I have gotten up for a while and then got back into bed, my heart rate would not restart at the low registered rate. It would start out higher and come back down as I relaxed. Frankly, I have NO CLUE. Watch malfunction? Sleepwalking? Astral travel? Participation in someone else's dream? Things that make you go, hmm.

38

DIVINE HELP – BE LIKE JANE!

Let me tell you about Jane*, who is my friend Stan's* mom. I met Jane many years ago. She was a tiny-but-mighty lady. She just knew her stuff. She was a protective nurturer as well. I gravitated to her as one of those energetic people you just want to sit and talk with when you can.

I will never forget one afternoon visiting her house. She was in the kitchen cooking and said she would be out in a minute!

I noticed Jane's Maltese puppy sleeping in the corner and was so excited! (I wanted one!) I crouched down and started calling the dog to come over so I could pet it. After the second time calling for the sleeping puppy, Stan's eyes got *REALLY WIDE,* and he whispered to me that their dog had passed away and that was the *taxidermy* version of it. Now, *my eyes* got really big. I was so embarrassed. I don't remember saying much for the rest of the visit. Ah, I digress.

As time passed, Jane got sick with throat cancer. I will never forget checking in on her and hearing her brag that she had some of the best doctors! She said they wrote her a prescription to eat Snickers candy bars and drink beer to try and put back on weight! Despite how she felt, she made an attempt to keep things lighthearted.

Eventually, her time on this earth ended. As a mentor of mine, it was hard for me. It was hard to see her physical body without its soul, but it didn't stop me from talking to her. I knew that she was around. She was just finally free of the pain that plagued her body.

The time came for Stan and his wife to sell her house. They contacted me to meet and make the proper arrangements to put it on the market. Her house was immaculate. It was in a great location, and I was honored and grateful to help. The first week I had listed it for sale, I had an open house. I set out my signs, turned the lights on, stood in the middle of her living room and talked out loud to her.

"Jane, Stan is ready to sell your house now that you don't need it anymore. You took such good care of your home, and I am asking for your help to bring in someone who will love and care for this as much as you did."

I then sat down, pulled out something to read, and waited. A short while later, a car pulled up. An agent and her client came in to look. I answered the questions they had about the house and the owner. The buyer really loved the house, and they went back to the office to write up an offer. I was excited! We negotiated a cash offer with Stan on the phone and made a deal. Cash, close in a week!

I closed up Jane's house, turned off all the lights, and again, standing in her living room said a heartfelt THANK YOU to Jane for her assistance.

The next day, I needed Stan to initial some of the formal paperwork, so I made copies and highlighted the areas that either needed initials or signatures. That's when I noticed it. The buyer's initials: *G.O.D.* I just stared. HOLY CRAP! HOW COOL IS THAT? I looked at the buyer's full legal name and sure enough, her initials were G.O.D.

I took the paperwork to Stan's business and told him that I prayed to his mom asking for her help, and she did indeed, help! (The first people who looked, cash offer, close in a week, no contingencies—rarely does it get any better than that!) I then showed him the bottom of the contract. You could see his eyes light up and he ran to the back to show his wife. His mom had touched him again as well.

The closing was seamless. Jane's gorgeous home was now in the hands of a new owner who loved and respected it as much as she did.

The buyer came up to me after the closing and said that she could feel the great energy in the house and that I was a good soul meant to do great things. There was an undeniable feeling, complete with goosebumps, that it was not only a message from her but from Jane. Goose bumps don't lie.

39

GHOST EMAIL FROM 1969?

So, THIS happened …

The backstory is that I had been getting a lot of messages about forgiveness. I have to forgive some people in my life for their transgressions. There was an instance of abuse that suddenly came to mind from a neighbor when I was younger. I have not thought about this instance or person FOR-EV-ER. Honestly it has not been on my radar at all whatsoever.

I decided to look up this neighbor. Why now? Why this person? Spirit gives you nudges at times. In fact, it can sometimes be conceived as a sort of spiritual to-do list. With me, spirit will not let something go until I address it. This was one of those moments. Of course, now that the internet is around, it affords anyone the opportunity to get their very own JUNIOR INVESTIGATOR badge. I put mine on and went to work! Agent 008, reporting for duty!

So, I am scooting around, actively looking to see what and where this person was and my phone dings with incoming email. I grabbed my phone and saw the email. It's an email dated from 1969! Talk about being in shock! Was I really seeing this correctly? Something told me to take a screenshot of it, which I did immediately! Was this a sign from the person I was looking up? I had no idea.

I sent the screenshot off to a few friends and started looking around for something that had to do with this person and the date of the email. Was one tied to the other? I discovered the person I was looking up passed away many years ago. So, what was the correlation between all of this, and did it have anything to do with the email?

I had to look this up, but the first emails were created in the early 1990s. The year AOL, Prodigy, and CompuServe all showed up was 1995. Hotmail didn't even start till 1996/1997. So, WHO SENT ME AN EMAIL FROM 1969?

NO SENDER, NO SUBJECT.

I was certainly intrigued for sure! I found no connection to the person I was looking up. Not the anniversary of their date of birth, or date of death.

As I was scooting along, something prompted me to google just the date: 12/31/69. What popped up? Other people who have received this "ghost email."

According to what I have read, others have also received it, some upward of ten at a time. There is no concrete explanation though. Conspiracy theorists claim that there is some sort of computer glitch or some random algorithm/coding that sends it. Sounds plausible, right? Hey, if some computer genius can hack into some major companies' websites, no doubt they could create this. What stands to be questioned is why more people aren't receiving them. Only random people at random times. Furthermore, why ME at the same time I am looking up someone whom I'm supposed to forgive on the computer?

I picked up my phone to look and open the email again and IT WAS GONE. Disappeared. Evaporated into thin air. Was it deleted by accident? I looked into my trash, and it was not there. It simply vanished. The only proof I had was the screenshot I took because I was nudged too.

I find the strong coincidence between this email and my search for someone I'm supposed to forgive strange and also intriguing, to say the least. So many other "signs" show up at times that nothing is that strange to me anymore. If nothing else, it was quite the conversation topic. It has not happened again since.

40

LOOK BOTH WAYS

S o this title came to me, and even though I didn't know what I
was supposed to write about it, I wrote it down as an intuitive
nudge to pay attention to.

Sometimes when you get a nudge all of the information isn't
given to you at the same time. It's important to just piece together
and stockpile what you get until it forms a clear picture. I don't know
about you, but I have a squirrel-brain mentality sometimes.
Multitasking is my middle name. So, while doing some Monday tasks
I pondered what the statement *look both ways* means to me.

For example, did spirit get toothpaste on your shirt, make you
stub your toe, and give you engine issues because they were
intentionally trying to make you late? Maybe! For those of us who
need to practice patience, of course, the answer is yes. But what you
didn't know was that a semi plowed through the same intersection
that you would've been at should it have been two minutes earlier.

Therefore, because you were not there, you were not involved in a car accident. Looking at it differently, was it an inconvenience or a blessing?

Thinking on this further I had this epiphany about my living arrangements. You see, I have always owned a house. It's been maybe one or two years in between ownership at times, but I have always prided myself on owning a house. Since moving back to Florida, the prices for rent and purchase skyrocketed. I realize it's going to take me a little while longer to accumulate the funds necessary to make a purchase again here in the area. But when you *look both ways*, what was the gift in all of this? Well by not having a house to take care of, I also did not have to cut the lawn (although I absolutely adore cutting the lawn and take pride in playing in my yard). I also have not had to deal with any home maintenance because of paying rent. It became someone else's burden. In a nutshell, a lot of responsibility was not put on my shoulders. Of course, with Hurricane Ian racing through my town, I also was not subjected to, nor had the financial burden of, repairing my house after immense damage in the area. So, looking both ways, I can honestly say that the gift of not having what I wanted when I wanted it was also another gift in and of itself.

While having a conversation with a friend over coffee one day, she mentioned that she felt inadequate because she did not have a significant other. She knew that this was a trigger she needed to work through and had yet to figure out why. I looked at her and I said, "Are you sure that being alone right now is negative? Look at it both ways! What about those friends who are just financially stuck and want to be out on their own? What about all of your friends who act like they're in a really great relationship, but you know the behind-the-scenes story of misery? I bet some of your friends would kill to have your freedom, to have the ability to go, do, and see things alone and just breathe. Looking at it both ways, you can choose what side of the fence to be on."

Now, when you're in a place of calm and peace, it's so easy to look both ways and say these things to somebody else. I get it. There will always be positives and negatives in all situations. Even if you can only see the negatives at the moment, sometimes when you look back, you see the positives. You just didn't get all the pieces or nudges at once to know the reason. You just knew you needed to discover the reasons. The positives like getting out of a crappy relationship so you can finally breathe again. Possibly getting fired from a toxic job situation only to realize that it was the job that was the problem, not you after all. The list can go on and on.

Dear Reader,

It's not easy to always look at things both ways all the time. I encourage you to try and see the silver lining. If you can't see it, ask somebody else if they can, and have them point it out to you. You might be surprised by what they see that you can't.

41

I Had a Trigger Conversation And Won

One of my dear friends is dealing with parents who need assistance from their adult children as they get older. Watching my friends deal with this makes me uber-grateful that my parents are completely independent. But let me tell you, I listen intently to my friends who are dealing with this for various reasons.

I'm sure that there are many stories that could one-up the other and I do speak about this with all due respect, but the parents become the children and the children become the parents. There's a level of frustration that is beyond measure in everybody's eyes that I listen to. I listen intently and summarize the possible options should I ever be in this situation in the future.

For example, I have one friend who has a parental figure who wants to drop a lot of money on these young whippersnappers if he gets attention from them. Then there are those who decide that they need gallon-jug amounts of Viagra and other enhancement drugs. Your mind thinks it's still younger, but your body is not. Who are we to say? I digress.

Anyway, I have a friend who is looking for a home for her divorced parents. Guess what? This is a two-for-one deal. The kids were buying one condo to move them both back in together after they had been divorced for many years already. Everybody is playing pass-the-parent and it's-your-turn-you-owe-me game and it is nonstop. I get whispered phone calls from many of these people pleading with me to rescue them (find them a property) and get the parents out of their house. It's interesting, funny, and sad all at the same time.

To boot, I have been told that this father has narcissistic tendencies. I went into it with my boundaries firmly in place and my plethora of knowledge ready to go. I was as ready as I would ever be. Now mind you, he reminds me of my ex in many ways. There was a little thorn in my side because of this reminder to begin with, but I always treat everybody with the utmost respect.

I have been getting an earful of the issues they were having with the parents. While we were walking around this property discussing the pros and cons of purchasing it, I watched the father open up and start eating a bag of chips in this house without a care in the world. The son, the evening before, complained to me how sloppy his father was and I could see his point.

While munching on chips, the father decides to rapidly fire questions for me to answer thus trying to discombobulate me. I think he was testing the waters to see where my boundaries were and whether he could take control and get me flustered. If you know me, it really is the wrong thing to challenge me on.

I let him ask his questions, and without skipping a beat or adjusting my eyes I mirrored him and rapidly fired answers back. He was trying to argue as to *why there were no scrape marks from the previous owners' plates in the cabinetry.* This was a good three-minute conversation about why I don't know the answer to this. I don't even know the seller!

All in all, I could probably share a lot of different examples, but none of them are that important. I just took a moment to pat myself on the back. This was triggering to me, and I handled it with grace and knowledge. I stood my ground. I was just so proud of myself. This man did indeed show a great deal of narcissistic characteristics. I saw the game and didn't play his way. I didn't give him the satisfaction of trying to aggravate me as he does his children. Task taken on, mission accomplished, pop quiz taken, and I passed.

42

PUT IT ON MY TAB

As readers we can often channel for ourselves but many times it is easier to be a sitter and let someone else read for us. I just did a reading for somebody who also channels herself. We have exchanged readings with each other in the past.

A lot of times it's a more objective view since they don't know all the details, twists and turns going on in our current life.

During the readings I do for others, there is often a menagerie of things that my spirit team gives me to relay. They are always unique for the person who is in front of me no matter who they are. My language works for them.

There are often words and terms that I repeat but honestly don't have any knowledge of. For her, I received "wormwood," which I know I've heard before, but don't have a clue what the properties are, or what it does. Another phrase for her that stuck out was *"Put it on our tab."* I think I was more shocked about this phrase than the sitter was! The fact that spirit told someone to put it on their tab but also that spirit HAD a tab to put it on. The next question was how do I get one of these tabs?

I thought it was fascinating that spirit said to do this. *Tell us how much you need, and we'll make sure that you get the money in some way, shape or form.* Simultaneously, in my mind's eye, I saw an angel off to the side with the proverbial finger up dictating to somebody saying those words.

Those were very cool words for spirit to speak. I have been getting a lot of very unique things that mean everything to the person I am working for that don't mean anything to me, but I have yet to have an angel say put it on my tab. That was a new one for me!

Toward the end of the reading was a reference to an emerging butterfly from its cocoon. Spirit reminded her that it was the strength the butterfly gains from the struggle of pushing fluids from its body into its wings that makes them strong and able to fly. Spirit further said that she was like a butterfly and will be stronger and better because of whatever struggle she was enduring.

I don't often remember details of readings that I give but this one had parts that stood out. It was as if spirit was also holding a mirror up to me to reflect on how I did this already and how strong I now was.

Spirit wanted to know if she had any further questions to ask of them. She asked if there was any further information regarding the **double mastectomy that she had had three days prior.**

Shut the front door! WHAT? Spirit never let on about this detail to me but gave her all the information she needed to know.

As I picked my jaw up off the floor, she smiled and said a lot of what was said referenced this situation.

I was so grateful that she shared this with me as I had no idea. Then I got confirmation in the form of goose bumps. Waves and waves of them rolled over me as another drop-in message for her came through. *She will be flying stronger and higher because of this. She will be on a stage giving a testament of how she found strength in what she was doing, where it came from, her feelings and her healing.*

All I could do was just stare at her like I was in a trance. Spirit further channeled the words: *That's what this experience is about. That's why you're not feeling super down about it. You are actually going to be sharing your experiences.*

She smiled at me and said that it made perfect sense. I asked her to please remember us little people when she makes it big! She giggled at that. I said this is why you need to work on your automatic writing and journaling that spirit is mentioning. Spirits telling me to tell you that it's these little instances that you need to write so you won't forget them. This is all part of what you will speak about going forward. She thanked me and said it made perfect sense.

We parted ways after the reading, and I needed to rehash what just happened. First of all, spirit told HER what she needed to hear, not me. They never let me know about this major surgery she just had. It also just stuck in my head over and over again: *Put it on my tab!*

It is a reminder to ask for help from spirit and to set our intentions for the outcome we would like. Let go and let spirit handle things. Let *them* bring you the guidance and assistance you need. They will take care of it for us. It doesn't always show up exactly how we want, or how we think it should be presented to us but inevitably we get everything that we need because we put it on spirit's tab.

43

WE MUST, WE MUST, WE MUST INCREASE OUR BUST!

I have said it before and will say it again. Spirit tattles on people and I am no exception to this rule. During one of our group's woo-woo meetings, spirit took advantage of the fact that two of the guys in our group were not able to join us for the evening.

Boy, did they let some personal information really come out among us gals. There was so much laughter between us during this exchange that we lost track of time. Talk about being sidetracked! The more we laughed the higher our vibration and energy level is to tap into spirit so it is a win-win for all of us. Frankly, we never know what spirit is going to say, or know how it is said. This always makes it interesting! My guides are hysterical and blunt to boot. I rarely get sugar-coated messages. That's what makes it fun whether you are the sitter or the reader!

I will give you a fair warning right now that if you are easily offended, please skip to the next chapter. I won't be mad!

This week's practice had to do with medical intuition. For this exercise, we took turns tapping into one person at a time for four to five minutes and scanning their body to relay a report. Depending on how many attend is how many different reports you get. The reports are often similar in nature but have different aspects.

Being the coordinator of said events, I always go last to be read for to make sure that everybody gets a turn. Jan* is somewhat new to our group but not to her abilities. She obviously hadn't worked with my guides much to know how they could be so the look of shock and exasperation on her face was absolutely priceless.

I could reach a general consensus with everybody in the group that *my* spirit guides are hysterically funny. They optimize their opportunities to phrase things or show pictures to those reading me to evoke smiles and giggles.

For a long time now, I've been getting reports that there is a male who shows up on my right-hand side in my energy. I have a few ideas about who this could be, but not enough information has been given to be definitive. Mentioning this makes sense as to the rest of the report I received.

The rest of the report was that I have some eye strain going on from being in front of the computer too long. I am sitting too much and need to walk around outside. I literally and figuratively need to let my hair down, work on my sacral chakra, and stretch more than I do. Basically, all things that are typical of somebody who sits in front of the computer for long periods of time. Nothing shocking to report.

Then Jan spoke up and said she got something else different than the rest of the reported items but didn't feel like she should say something like this. She further explained that she was shocked that she would even get this word and was embarrassed.

Obviously, we are all dying to know at this point! So, one of the other girls spoke up and said *Lisa's guides are hysterical, if you receive something you need to repeat it as it is something she needs to hear!* Frankly her expression about whatever she received was funny in and of itself to say the least. *How bad could it be?*

Yeah, remember I said that.

Jan reported that my sacral chakra needed to be stretched and they wanted me to be a little bit more limber and I needed more (wait for it) ***orgasms***. Yes, spirit told me through my friends that I needed more orgasms.

No one could stop laughing at this point. I couldn't breathe and neither could anybody else in our group. We all were *so* happy that none of the guys were able to show up for the evening because the conversation would've definitely been a lot different.

You heard it right. Spirit tattled on me that I need to be more limber than I am for this mystery man stepping forward. They obviously know of some upcoming acrobatics in the bedroom! I'm grateful for the heads-up but they better not watch!

So as the conversations went on and the laughter finally died down it was confirmed by other people that they also got like kind messages for me to get out, have fun and so on. I was grateful as I have been working way too much lately.

Another skilled person in our group doodles when she gets information from spirit and draws words and pictures. While discussing her drawings, Jan was very impressed with them asking to see more. Looking at one of a woman she blurted out that she wished her boobs were as big as hers in the drawing.

Of course, that's all it took, and laughter erupted all over again! These are absolutely not normal conversations we were having but spirit had us in rare form! Jan is a beautiful slender woman but felt she lacked in the chest department.

Through our laughter, I suggested that we could do some of those old-time chest exercises. I kid you not, simultaneously and without skipping a beat, we all put palms together in front of our chest squeezing our pectoral muscles chanting, *We must, we must, we must increase our bust.* This alone set us into another fit of giggles. There was not a dry eye in the group!

As a friendly reminder not only does spirit tattle on you, but no subject is off-limits. If a message is meant for you, you will get it one way or the other. I am just grateful that my spirit guides have a comedic side. Their delivery is priceless!

44

Ms. Wanna-Fix-It Is at It – Again

Spirit has made me very aware of my constant offering of extra energy to people, places, and circumstances of late. Once again, I have taken vague statements spoken as being an implied desire for my help. I don't know why I can't get this through my thick head. *Every comment or statement is not a plea to bail someone out or fix their life or issue.* I just assume that it is, and we all know what the word assume means! Sadly, this is not my first rodeo about being like this. Spirit needs me to be super aware and curtail this no matter how it is wrapped or presented to me. I think I know why, too.

Seeing this pop up again for me to address has been frustrating. True to spirit style, if you don't figure it out and learn the lesson, you will keep doing it with the same results just wrapped differently. That's what happened: The same issue was wrapped differently, and I fell for it. Failing more than a few pop quizzes in this department, spirit has issued me a tutor in the form of spiritual nudges to pay attention to this issue, again.

Repeat after me: *I need to not offer my unasked-for opinion, offer unsolicited solutions, buy unnecessary or unwanted things in the name of "help."*

There's just been a string of things that spirit has been reminding me of very consistently. I have felt stopped dead in my tracks with the message, *Were you asked?* Ninety-nine percent of the time the answer was a resounding no.

I have realized how much grief, time, energy and wasted resources I have potentially saved by asking myself this question at the nudging of spirit. The bigger question is why do I keep doing this?

I had to sit with this a bit.

Where did it stem from? I'm pretty sure it is rooted back to childhood. You know the saying, *Do unto others as you would have them do unto you.* To me, if you had to be asked, you didn't want to do it in the first place. Then of course being programmed by my environment that in order to receive I needed to give more than 5,000,000 percent. I am sure there is some codependency mixed in all of this as well. I'm not sure if I am feeding or breeding it. Then let's slap on being a recovering people pleaser. Do I need to go on? UGH.

I do realize that my attention and time in situations is often enough. *I am enough.* It's not that I am asked to come along because I am expected to fix or buy anything. My energy and attention are my calling card. I don't have to be involved or immersed in other people's situations or experience.

Newsflash! If someone vents or talks about something it probably means they are working through it on their own and they just want you to listen. *SHHH!*

Obviously, this has been a lesson for me that I will need to keep working on. I think I am getting a bruise from all the nudging from spirit on this subject.

The other lesson in all of this is to be shown how someone values me. Do they always want or expect something from me? I need to see for myself in what capacity I am showing up in other people's lives. You'll see exactly who is expecting things from you and who is not.

My Ms. Wanna-Fix-It toolbelt needs to be retired!

Dear Reader,

Believe it or not, this is not only about minding your own business but pulling back your precious energy from others. We often are blinded by the immense amounts of effort we put forth for people thinking we are helping and yet we are only sacrificing ourselves. Remember to pause. Be mindful if you were asked for help or assistance or to just hold space for them while they figure it out. You may be surprised by the answer!

45

SCRAMBLED BRAIN CELLS – HIGH ENERGY

Do you ever have days where chunks of time seemingly evaporate?

Currently, there is a prediction of a hurricane hitting the area that I am currently residing in, Florida. Of course, we're still a few days out. But there's this panic that sets in among everyone whether spoken or unspoken. It is survival of the fittest. There were long lines at the gas station today. Long lines for people stocking up on propane for grills, and I saw plenty of plywood in the back of trucks for those people needing to board up their windows.

I went with some friends last night out to play drag queen bingo. It was a tremendous amount of fun just to get out and hang out with the girls despite what was going on with the weather. It has been mentioned to me more than I care to admit recently that I need to get out and do fun things. So, when the offer came, I went.

I also want to stress that I have right now what I call the "IT" factor in the last few days. Spirit calls it shining your light. I have tried to quietly not draw attention to myself but some days, it's like a lighthouse light. Everybody notices you. It would almost be in the same order of walking around in a clown suit or being buck-naked where everybody seems to pay attention. Although I assure you. I had all my clothes on, and I was not in a clown suit.

I went to the grocery store to grab a handful of things, and I had people stopping me to talk and men who were blatantly checking me out. Anyway, it's been a while since I have had that feeling. Honestly, I mostly ignore all of that stuff, so maybe it was just that I was aware of it this time? That I don't know.

I think part of it is that my energy was just on point I felt empowered at the moment, and I actually did something with

my hair.

As we do when storms potentially are in the vicinity, we watch the local weather for the latest spaghetti plots. The energy around me was heightened though. The minute I started to focus or overthink anything it felt like spirit scrambled my brain. Every time! If I tried to focus on anything that had to do with the storm or think about the next day, my brain scrambled again. It didn't matter how much I tried to multitask. I was only allowed to do one thing at a time. Scrambling to me is like someone quickly flipping through radio stations in my head. Not fun.

I realized that spirit was really enforcing the fact they did not want me to worry or think about tomorrow or the storm. I needed to be present for the day. That was my only job. When I finally figured this out, well at least attempted to, that's when I saw the feather in my path. To me it was like spirit saying, *Thank you*!

I was also getting repetitive nudges to get a reading done for myself. I declared three objects as signs to get answers from my spirit guides and angels. One for the answer yes get a reading, one for no, and one for ask a different question. As always, I typed an email to myself through my phone with a deadline to produce either a word or picture of the established signs and got the sign within seven minutes. I knew that spirit had a message for me and with the high energy around, I was not getting it. When I was done, there was another feather in my path. I love getting signs!

But my point is that today felt like a hot mess with my head being scrambled and chunks of time evaporating. I got home from my errands, and I decided to give myself a mental break because it was just overwhelming. I think I was picking up on the hyper-anxious energy in the air because people were working to take care of things in case this hurricane hit us. Gotta love being an empath! Did I remember to put a bubble of protection around me? Nope. Lesson learned.

Dear Reader,

If you are going to be any place with a lot of people or intense energy, simply ask spirit to place a bubble of protection around you. This helps so incredibly much. Often, you will leave the place feeling fine instead of being drained. It's worth it!

46

THE CALM BEFORE THE STORM

There is a mutiny going on inside my head, and not one thought or idea is standing out above the others. Yet around me everything is calm. Hurricane Ian is going to make landfall where I live. It makes a difference if it is a direct hit or if you are on the left or right of the storm. Being on high alert and analyzing everything is exhausting. I need a nap.

Both of my kids also live within the cone where this hurricane could hit but are four-plus hours apart. Both have new babies. I can't be everyplace at once to help. Both of them want to hold down their own homestead, which I get. Let me just say that this mamma bear wants to help and protect both of them and is floundering about how to do it.

On top of that, my mom and her husband are in the cone of being hit after us as well. She had heart surgery scheduled at a hospital that is also in line with where landfall will occur. Luckily the doctors canceled it, but it didn't cancel the need.

Spirit continued to remind me that everything would be fine, and my only job was to take care of myself. I was to be *the calm inside the storm,* literally and figuratively. How? Good question. I am in superwoman mode. Ready to leap tall buildings in a single bound!

Here comes the airplane lecture about how I am to take care of myself first and let everybody else take care of themselves. I know that is the correct answer but as a mom and a superhero, I want to jump in and be everybody's everything. I want to be an extra set of hands, a calming voice, the nurse, the provider, and I'm not really wanted or needed anywhere right now. So, I watch the never-ending loop of weather reports to see if anything has changed in the storm's trajectory.

While on mental autopilot, spirit continues to bring to my attention the messages in the past readings for me. A big one is that *the only validation I will have about some situations is after they have occurred.* I have been told that there is a tower moment coming. I will need to rebuild but ultimately, I'm going to be fine. Is this it? Will this hurricane hit and wipe everything out that I have just rebuilt and unpacked? Then, I had a dream a couple of nights ago about prepping because tornadoes were dropping out of the sky. This is before the storm was even predicted to come to the area or was a named storm. So, based on just those two bits of information is something going to happen and wipe everything out?

A great conversation piece is to ask others what is the most important thing to them that they would grab should there be a natural disaster? Mine has always been my family photos. Those are snapshots of time that I could never replace or duplicate. I gave thought to what else I could possibly want and what popped up was my dream journal and my notebook of readings and channeling that I have done for myself. It's almost like a Nostradamus type of book to me. Of course, there are miscellaneous things that I would grab, but nothing that would be bulky at all.

But my point is that I just have to take care of myself, and I'm not used to doing that in this capacity. There's always been a focus on other things.

The concern for the loss of life around me and the message about there being a spear through my heart, also come to mind.

I recently received a message about something to do with being hit by lightning. This could be something or somebody around me that would be hit. Is this literal or metaphorical?

You know in one regard not talking out loud about any of this helps to keep it under wrap. This is something that I feel the need to talk about though. I am *always* the strong one for everyone else and veer away from speaking of my fears to others. They lean on *me*; I don't lean on others.

In another regard, there's been so much told to me about my future going forward that if I honestly had to walk away from everything again, I would be OK. I've only had all my stuff back for a few months to begin with.

Yesterday the energy seemed high around me, and spirit was chatting upside down and backward. I don't know if I was hearing the thoughts of everybody else, but they were random messages.

At this point, all I can do is wait like everyone else. I am not bigger, better, stronger, or smarter than the storm approaching. It doesn't matter how much I worry, fret, cry, or get upset. I cannot fix anything. It doesn't matter what direction I go. Spirit just wants me to have faith that it will be OK and that my family and I are protected. I will trust and believe.

47

SEPTEMBER 28, HURRICANE IAN

Hurricane Ian, Category 4/5 storm
September 28, 2022

Over the years I have had many people ask why would you live in Florida and deal with hurricanes? To answer that question, it is simple. It is often five to seven days coming, a good two or three days until a better view of the "cone of certainty" and then, well, we see what happens. You get little to zero warning for earthquakes or tornados. I get the concern even more now. This time, we weren't so lucky.

The inside scoop on living here is when there is a name storm headed in our direction the energy shifts among the natives. You have those who are uber-prepared, restocking supplies, filling up the gas tanks and taking precautions. Then you have the groups that don't think anything is going to happen. Maybe to describe those people better is more of the "last-minute" prep people. I tell everyone in a blanket statement, whatever you do or do not do, you're either going to be really right or really wrong. The scoreboard and running total have been in favor of the ones who do nothing.

The running joke is that being a weatherperson in the area is the only job you can have where you can be wrong so often and keep your job. In defense of them the weather forecasters are damned if they overtalk about something and damned if they don't. They truly are damned if they don't make a big deal about it and damned if they do. They can't win. I will tell you though that everyone keeps one eye glued to the local television station of their choice.

This was one time they were right and the area I am in got hit. My heart, prayers and healing were sent multiple times a day to all those who sustained irreparable damage and will forever be scarred by this experience.

As much as it would have been, to find something funny about this hurricane would be disrespecting those who suffered great loss. I still cannot bring myself to go to the island beaches that took such a guttural hit and see for myself in person what is no longer there.

That being said, there were most certainly some highlights of this experience from my neck of the woods.

First of all, earlier that year while babysitting my granddaughter, my son decided it would be a great idea to replace the windows with impact-resistant ones and replace the roof while I was there babysitting. Both were done over the summer and there had to be no air conditioning on while they worked. I could see the slightest twinkle in his eye when I point-blank asked if this was done on purpose to which he smirked and said, no. Overall, it wasn't something I would have volunteered for. All the strange people in and around the property made the dog anxious, and me being highly empathic did NOT help.

One afternoon, while the workers were there, the energy was exceptionally wonky for some reason. Not being able to use sage and clear the home, I gave myself a self-imposed time-out. I sat on the end of the couch, put on a ten-minute meditation and told my son's dog and my granddaughter that *Mimi needs a time out and we were going to all meditate*! I then closed my eyes to seek my calm and centered place again. The funniest thing happened. The dog came over and put his paw on my leg and my granddaughter rolled over to me and she reached out and touched my leg as well. Frankly it was wild to me that they did this, but I was not arguing!

So fast forward to the warning of the weather department on the news that Hurricane Ian shifted. It was now headed straight for us. I still had supplies that had traveled to North Carolina and back. I had a to-go bag and my supplies ready. My photos were triple-layered in garbage bags and then put in Rubbermaid tubs up off the ground for safekeeping. My phones, extra battery packs and laptops were kept fully charged and I watched the news like everyone else.

I finally went to bed at 11:30 p.m. only to be woken up by my son calling me at 2:30 a.m. and saying, *It's getting bad, Mom, you need to come over here, NOW*.

I took one last look at my "stuff," locked my door and headed toward my son and daughter-in-law's house. Driving away I didn't know what or if there was going to be anything left when I came back.

While driving, I spoke out loud to spirit and asked that a bubble of protection be placed around my and my son's home. My son met me in the driveway and helped me unload my supplies and park my car to help avoid flying debris.

I lay down on the couch and tried to go back to sleep. My phone started going off the hook about 5 a.m. A client's daughter had left Canada, avoided Hurricane Fiona and made it into the area before the airports were shut down here in Florida. She was at their vacation home in my area and not answering her phone. Of course, watching the continuing coverage, they were super concerned and asked me to try and reach her. The home she was in was literally one street away from the river. It was expected to have a massive storm surge. I assured them I would and would keep them posted as much as possible while we still had electricity and phones. I realized that once upon a time, I would have sacrificed myself and the car to drive over there and check. I didn't this time.

Since I was up, I said more prayers and also prayed that the new roof and impact windows would keep us all safe. Spirit obviously knew what was going on for there to be encouragement for my son and his wife to start those projects. (Sneaky buggers!)

Although I did not have any premonitions about this storm in my dreams, there have been other metaphorical events I could claim to be part of this. What I did know is all the future premonitions that have not yet happened. Things in the future that were still to play out for me and my granddaughter. I found peace in that. It was not a guarantee of a smooth or bumpy ride, but I had faith we would get through it.

My mom and her husband were further inland and kept us posted via news outlets since the power went off and we had no TV or Internet. They were going to possibly get hit after us, depending on how the wind shifted the massive storm.

There are many details that would bore you, but I will just share the highlight reel. First, my grandson was barely six weeks old and being breastfed. Lucky little guy slept through everything despite it being super warm inside after the power went out. Being warm did not help the ever-building tension in the house.

My son, daughter-in-law and I wandered window to window reporting what was going on and what now was flying through the air. We took bets on when the neighbor's trampoline would officially take flight. We watched lakes appear in the streets with whitecaps. We saw flying objects pierce the ground. Sections of roofs and fences became flying projectiles. Chunks of trees were bouncing off the roof like tumbling weeds.

We all had our eyes and ears open, and the tension was intensified as the storm just sat over us for what seemed like eternity.

Then the smoke alarms started going off. **ALL of them**. It was such a wimpy noise coming from them and my son looked at me and said what is that? I said, *"Those are your smoke alarms! Guess what you're getting for Christmas this year?"* My son grabbed a flashlight, and we ran to each scuttle hole for the attic and checked each room for a fire or smoke. We saw and smelled nothing.

A bit later while looking out the back windows of the house we saw flames at a house some streets away even with the high winds and rain. We were helpless to do anything. No fire or police service was allowed to be out until the storm was over. All we could do was hope and pray that everyone there was finding another place of refuge. The winds were sustained at 100 to 140 miles per hour. No one was safe to leave the house. We later learned that they were in an upstairs closet and had a tea light in a closet that ignited. It felt awful to feel helpless.

The storm was extremely slow, and we all lost cell phone usage for many hours. Since the towers went down, all we had was SOS mode. Because of the lack of power and internet, we didn't know what was going on or where. All we knew was the damage we could see out our windows.

We discussed where the birds and outdoor animals find refuge during a storm. Trees are not safe. Going underground was not an option because of the rain and flooding as well. This conversation was spurred on because of this one squirrel that decided to dash across the yard to the edge of the street—now turned lake running to or from something. We all wanted to run out and save him! We don't know where he went but we cheered him on!

When we finally saw the storm leave and we could open the house, it felt like the scene from *The Wizard of Oz* when Dorothy comes out of the house except, we didn't see everything in color. We saw devastation. Roofs were gone, debris was everywhere, patio cages were wrapped over the top of people's houses, trees were toppled over, and cars were damaged. The cleanup began and neighbors banded together to help one another. I said thank you over and over again to spirit that all of us were unscathed and the house was minimally damaged. Of course, that was just one house. Many, many other homes and businesses were not so lucky.

I gave hugs to everyone and headed back to see what and if there was anything left of my place. It was further south than where my son lived and surrounded by canals. My place was older and not up to the most current hurricane codes and standards for the area. I had no idea what I was going home to—if anything. There were traffic lights you had to literally drive around so they didn't smack your car. There were boats in the road, light poles laying across streets, trees twisted every which way and electrical lines strewn everywhere. Frankly horrific devastation was all around on the drive, yet I knew I had not seen the worst of it.

I pulled up to my place and my neighbors' condo and the surrounding condos had cages collapsed in, screens were gone, windows on some of the surrounding buildings were blown out and roofs were gone with patio furniture literally dangling off the edge of the upstairs patios. I parked my car, went inside and saw no visible damage. For as old and thin as the windows were, shockingly they had not blown in. The palm trees right next to my unit had not collapsed onto my space. There was no water intrusion that I could see except some water on the sills from driving rain. The little space I finally could call my own was spared. My neighbor and surrounding condos were not so fortunate.

I again spoke out loud and thanked spirit for keeping that which was around me safe. I was insanely grateful and kept saying thanks. I questioned if the reason I didn't have my pod back was to get used to having nothing. I didn't find myself attached to anything specific except my family photos and videos.

The energy of others from the storm damage was so thick and palpable you could cut it like a knife. Actually, it was so heavy if it had been literal, I would have needed a chainsaw.

I did my best to protect my energy by only chatting minimally. I checked on friends and family when we had cell service by temporary towers for one hour a day. I got my crayons and coloring books out, made a peanut butter and jelly sandwich, listened to music on my phone and rinsed off in the pool for a bath while the water was still chlorinated. As much as I wanted to jump in and help other neighborhoods, we were all advised to stay home. Military personnel and first responders were out, and they didn't need any further complications from accidents involving those wanting to help or just be nosey.

The days that followed were a blur. Everyone chipped in to clean up and make repairs in our own areas. Our cars that weren't damaged became very expensive charging stations for our phones and electronics. There were military helicopters and personnel in town picking stranded people off the surrounding waterlogged islands and bringing them to safety and issuing supplies. It was horribly disheartening to hear story after story. One was always worse than the next. I think it was in some ways a gift that we didn't have Internet or electricity for nine days in my area. It also prevented us from seeing online or on television what the world was watching. We were prevented from seeing the devastation of what actually happened in other surrounding areas. Again, being empathic, I know it was for my protection. It was also surreal to see and hear life going on in other parts of the world with those of us here left to pick up the pieces and go on. It made me realize that I have been that person going on with my life as devastation has hit other areas and people's lives.

I have always been (in my opinion) calm in a storm. I didn't realize how important it truly was until that time frame. I didn't react. I just responded. Everyone had their own mental burdens to deal with. I loaned my strength and support to those that needed it but remembered to keep a hefty reserve for myself.

I had someone out of state request a reading from me prior to the storm and I told her I didn't know when I would be back up and running as she was in a northern state. She prayed for me and checked up on me when I could finally respond.

Again, there are many, many stories about this, but I wanted to share as it was important to reflect on where my mental state and gifts were at times going forward.

48

SHOULD I STAY OR SHOULD I GO?

S ince the hurricane, there have been a lot of displaced workers who help our seasonal residents at local food and beverage establishments. One of our fellow high school business owners, along with other businesses, decided to do an outdoor fundraiser to help. So many people were happy to help a cause and do something more upbeat and normal. The plans were set in motion. The date and time were set, and our friend group volunteered to run a face-painting booth. It wasn't much, but it was something.

We showed up and listened to other fellow high school friends play in the band. It felt great to do something for a cause on a sunny afternoon.

I was sitting next to my friend Angie*, and we were discussing the band and how they had changed the name recently. She brought up that her dad used to play the *banjo*. *I* sat there, looking at her, and I said what instrument did you say again? She said a *banjo*.

You see, prior to showing up to this fundraiser, I had asked spirit that if it was in my best interest to go back to Hogwarts (the Arthur Findlay College of spiritualism and psychic sciences in England) to show me a banjo, in a word or picture. If the answer was to not go right now, show me a bow and arrow, in a word or picture by bedtime the next evening. I immediately picked up my phone and showed Angie the email that I had sent to myself. She just looked at me and said, *"Are you kidding me?"* I said nope! I thanked her for allowing spirit to give me the answer through her. She was just as much in awe as I was. I had it in writing after all. I'm actually really excited to brush up on a few skills. Even though the departure

was only a few months away, it put a fire under me to get further projects done.

For me it was the cherry on top to get confirmation to go again. It made the day even better. To boot, the goal to raise money for these displaced workers was about $2,000. In total before we had finished, there was over $25,000. Spirit was helping all of us!

49

BACK TO HOGWARTS

The Arthur Findlay College, Stansted, England,

Part 1: THE TRIP

Postcard

Spirit brought to my attention that my life has been very calm and void of moments that I would shake my head at lately. It's been kind of nice actually! I could see and tell that this trip was going to give me more stories to tell and to take everything in my stride.

My decision to go back to Hogwarts was really founded for a few different reasons. Primarily I just want to be better at my gifts. I have pretty high expectations for myself. Going back to school sounded like the best thing for me. I also was in need of a change of scenery and pace. Just the trip to and from England was worthy of the statement: *You can't make this shit up*! So, my adventures are about the traveling part of the trip and then the course itself. This postcard is about traveling there and back. It was one thing after another, and it was so far-fetched I had to write it down!

When I got the sign from spirit that it was OK to go to England again, I compiled all of my airline points that were going to expire and purchased a round-trip ticket to England.

As the time to pack drew nearer, the notes I took from the last trip paid off. I had a folder of notes that I had accumulated prior to going. Added to that were the new notes from being there prior. All of this was extremely helpful! Things like remembering to take a lanyard for your keys so you can hang them around your neck. Other details like taking an extra bag to carry your clean clothes and toiletries for the bathroom. It made me very happy reading all these hints, tricks and reminders. The extra effort to write after my last trip paid off. I was grateful because it helped make things easier as I didn't have to think so much.

The class I was taking started the Monday after our Thanksgiving holiday here in the United States, so I needed to travel like a lot of other people over the weekend. If you've ever traveled over a holiday weekend, you know it takes a lot of patience. I figured since I was flying it wouldn't be that bad right? Not!

For starters, the local news reported that there was absolutely zero parking available in the short- or long-term parking lots at the airport. It was suggested that if you wanted to come to the airport, whether to take a flight or pick someone up, you needed to find other methods of transportation. I was still one day ahead of my scheduled flight, so I started looking around to make other arrangements and had something else lined up. I woke up on Saturday, the second day after Thanksgiving, and they announced that there were open spaces available. Phew!

I got to the airport a little early considering this was an international flight. This was my first flight since COVID. I wasn't sure what to expect. I wanted to be extra prepared, so I got myself there a little bit early. Everything went swimmingly well. I knew my way around. The first stop was going to be Charlotte, North Carolina.

Here's where it started to get interesting. Honestly, I would suggest getting a bowl of popcorn and a drink so that if you snorted it, and it came out your nose, it wouldn't burn. Yes, it was that kind of a trip.

The plane lands in Charlotte, North Carolina, as the first stop. Given that this was an international flight from Charlotte to London, there were lots of people with lots of foreign accents who I truly just gravitated to. I just love listening to them talk around me.

There were plenty of us waiting at the gate. Nothing was happening. No one knew what was going on really. The gate people had masks and offered a few whispered announcements that no one could understand. So finally, after shaking our heads and asking one another, *Did you hear that? Did you hear that?* I announced to the people around me *I got this!*

I marched up to the people at the ticket counter. I informed them that I was the official representative of the peanut gallery in the back. I told them that no one could understand or hear what they were saying. I asked if they would please be so kind as to repeat to me what they said so that I could repeat it to those around me instead of having everybody individually come up and ask them. They repeated what they wanted to say. Me and my big mouth literally turned around and announced to everybody who could not hear what they said. Basically, our plane was having mechanical difficulties, and they were working on trying to fix them. There was a delay because of this.

People shouted back, "*Thank you*," and I actually had a few people clap so then I resumed my position at the back of the peanut gallery. My big girl britches were pulled up tightly under my chin!

After waiting a while longer with no further update, I decided it was probably in my best interest to go get something to eat. No one knew how long before the flight was going to take off. Kudos to my spirit team for *that* intuitive nudge!

Two hours later they finally came back on the loudspeaker and announced that the plane needed to be sent back to the hangar for repairs. They found us another plane that could get us to JFK Airport in New York where there would be a better-equipped plane that would take us across the Atlantic Ocean. They apologized for the inconvenience. I don't think a lot of us minded as long as we were moving.

We all piled into the new plane and buckled up. An hour and a half later we were now at JFK. It was now 10:30 p.m. We all unloaded and waited for instructions at the gate again. The instructions that never came. We're waiting, stall stall stall, *Oh, the plane is here*, stall stall stall. *Oh, we have to wait for the flight attendants*, stall stall stall, *Now we are waiting for the pilot*, stall stall stall. *Now we have to wait for the concessions to be loaded onto the plane* and so on and so on and so on. Basically, nothing was happening fast.

There were absolutely no vendors open in JFK as it was now *2 a.m.* There are 211 of us waiting. I was around people who were trying to get to Dubai, Australia, the Netherlands, and Germany, just to name a few. None of these people could even make arrangements for connecting flights, because they didn't know when they were going to get us out of JFK.

The natives were getting restless. Somebody said out loud, *"Can somebody at least get us some water off of the plane. There's absolutely nothing to drink. There're no water fountains and all the vendors are closed in the airport."* Someone finally got on the plane and brought out bottles of water for everybody.

There was more grumbling among us passengers. One of the ladies sitting by me who was going to Germany came back from the counter with vouchers. Although not making a formal announcement to avoid a mad rush, they were giving vouchers for food concessions *when the airport reopened.*

Now, closer to 3 a.m., they had FINALLY announced that they would not be able to get us off the ground as they first thought and that the next flight they could promise us was 9:30 a.m. NOW there was a mad rush of people going to the counter to try to get hotel accommodation and driver concessions.

Although it sounded nice to get a driver to take us to a local hotel and get a room, it simply didn't make sense for such a short period of time. About 110 of us were all thinking the same thing. It wasn't worth it to leave and try and get back into the airport and through security with it still being a holiday weekend.

Let me just tell you, I said, *Hell-to-the-no*! For those of us who stayed and refused to leave the terminal, they brought airplane blankets and pillows off the plane for us to sleep on the floor of JFK. The armrest didn't go up on the chairs, so the floor was the only option if you didn't want to sleep sitting up. I know that there's a Tom Hanks movie about him sleeping in a terminal and I'm sure a lot of other movies. Personally, this was a new experience for me. I took it in my stride and found what I felt was the cleanest piece of carpet to somehow close my eyes and rest. It had been a very long day so far, and I hadn't even made it to England, which is five hours ahead in time.

When my alarm went off, I was not upset as I was sleeping on the cold floor next to a window during winter in New York. This Florida girl was not dressed for winter. I went and got some much-needed coffee, since the vendors were starting to open up and waited patiently like everyone else. The information we were receiving about the new plane and time had now dwindled down to nothing. Eventually, we did make it onto the plane.

There was a lady who was supposed to sit in my row on the aisle. She moved to the row in front of me as no other patron had sat there yet. She wanted a window seat but paid for an aisle. She was being somewhat rude to the stewardess about her desires. I didn't mind as I was going to have the whole row to myself. I had my earphones packed and my phone charged and was ready to go until they had in-flight entertainment. Once we had reached cruising altitude, the lady in front of me decided to recline her seat back. It is normally not a problem, but it was hitting my knees, and the TV screen was probably about a foot away from my eyes. It was not a big deal until she moved to the center seat and never put the seat next to the window back upright. I finally tapped her on the shoulder and asked her if she would please be so kind as to put her seat back in the upright position to which she said you should've said something sooner. Of course I had a few choice words to say but at this point I was tired, showed grace and said nothing.

I normally travel to England a day early to account for the time change. The extra day and the fiasco with the airlines served me well. I should have arrived at 7 a.m. on Sunday morning. I had a hotel set up for me for the evening of Sunday too. Classes started on Monday morning. The flight landed at 11:45 p.m. Sunday. I was very grateful for my prebooked hotel accommodation. I went to the taxi counter at the airport as it was the only place open and asked them to call me a ride to my hotel.

Of course, ten minutes to them was thirty minutes long but a gentleman finally arrived to drive me. He picked me up in a new Jaguar. Now I'm no slouch, but I was pretty impressed. He dropped me off.

I went to the gentleman at the front desk of my hotel and gave them the reservation number. He escorted me up to my room, which said *executive suite*. I do not remember booking an executive suite, but I was not going to argue. I was overly tired and was grateful for a bed instead of a floor.

I made it to Hogwarts (Arthur Findlay College) on time. PHEW!

Going home, the trip was just as eventful. I decided I was going to take the bus from Stansted Airport back to London Heathrow. I had the taxi pick me up promptly at 7:30 a.m. from the college. I had everything 100 percent ready to go. When I got there though, I had missed the bus. The next bus was going to get me to the airport much too late for my comfort. I didn't want to push my luck so the bus people mentioned I could take the train. They gave me three different changes I would need to take to use the rail system. I think the look on my face gave me away. I didn't have nearly enough coffee in me to mentally remember what they said. They commented and said you're not from around here, are you? I said no, I'm not. I'm sure I had the illustrious deer in headlights look. They recommended that I take a taxi and gave me directions to go back to the airport. I was to go to the third floor and go to the taxi hub. OK, no problem, right?

Ha! You would think! I got into the elevator, pressed the button for the floor that I needed and wouldn't you know the elevator doors would not open. Yes, you heard me right, I am now stuck in the elevator. OK, I've seen this before in movies. Thinking about what other people have done, I go to the doors and attempt to pry them open. Did it work? Not a bit. I decided to look up, thinking if my alternate escape was going to be crawling through the ceiling and realized I couldn't reach the ceiling, even if I stood on my suitcase. So, of course, I did what any other sane person would do and pressed the emergency button. I continued to repeatedly press the open-door button to no avail. It had been a few minutes. Someone finally answered and asked me what the issue was, and I said *I'm stuck in the elevator,* and they said OK and that they "will try to find somebody" to get me out.

I don't know if I necessarily liked the words *were going to try and find somebody.* Obviously, this doesn't happen too often but at this point it was a good eight or nine minutes while I just stood there. All I could do was laugh. I became very aware that I hadn't had these kinds of situations happen to me recently as it had been very calm and mundane. There hadn't been any *you can't make this shit up* moments for a while. Yet here I was being presented with new material on a silver platter! OK, it was a silver elevator, but you get the point.

Finally, somebody was able to rescue me from the elevator and I walked to the taxi counter like nothing happened. This was a very reputable company that I have used before but $220 for a one-and-a-half-hour drive was still a little pricey. Still with no coffee in me, I wasn't going to look a gift horse in the mouth. I was finally in route to the airport.

The flight back to the States was uneventful. I watched *Harry Potter* movies while they served us meals, snacks, wine, and ice cream! Yes, ice cream on the airplane! That was new for me! After we landed in Charlotte, North Carolina, we were cattle-herded to the customs area, being an international flight. I swear six airplanes deboarded all at the same time. So-many-people. They shuffled us to an escalator into a basement area where customs officials were waiting for us. With all the people we were seriously packed to the gills. Honestly, we were all taking steps in cadence and rhythm with the person in front of us.

As the end of the escalator was approaching, we seemed to be anticipating that last step onto the landing in front of us. The gentleman in front of me took a step forward. I also took a step forward in alignment with his step except *his shoelace had become untied and got caught in the escalator!* He tripped going forward. The step I took was going to make me fall on top of him! My fancy footwork and I rolled off of him onto the landing as his shoelace that was caught was being pulled back down into it by the teeth. Jolted, the people behind me surmised what was going on and saw the terror of the man in front of me who was now facing the people behind him as he was being pulled back toward the escalator. Somebody grabbed the man under his arms, someone else grabbed the guy's leg that had his shoelace caught and someone else was looking for an emergency stop button of which there was none. The people behind me worked to get his shoelace unstuck or detached before being chewed up. People behind them had to continue moving off the escalator. I lost track of where the man was.

You would think this is where the story ends but wait! There's more!

Now there is a one-and-a-half-hour zigzag line to approach the customs agents. There were only three available agents working for the night at the time we were there. I had my mask on to not catch any foreign cooties from anyone and just looked around. There were people from Turks and Caicos and a lot of people from other sunny destinations who had flip-flops on and the most fabulous, glowing tans. I kept looking at myself thinking, *Wow I live in Florida and I'm not even that tanned!*

It was finally my turn to go up to the customs agent. At this point I had officially hit the wall with my energy. I was not only super tired, but slaphappy. I say slaphappy, because of the next words that rolled off my tongue. (Just keep that in mind for the next part.) I approached the agent, and he asked me to take my mask off so they could take a picture. He reviewed my passport, then asked what was the nature of my business going to England? I kid you not, without skipping a beat, I looked him in the eyes, and said, *I went to go talk to dead people.*

You should have seen the wide-eyed shock in his eyes while simultaneously moving his hand toward the gun on his hip. Without skipping a beat, he said, "*Excuse me?* I looked at him very deadpan and said, "*I'm a psychic medium. I went to college in England to practice talking to dead people.*" He gestured very curiously that I needed to explain this a bit more to him. I told him that family members or friends can step forth from the other side, and I have the ability to retrieve messages from them and pass them along to you. I further explained that there is a college in England that I attend and it's one of many things I can do.

I don't think he knew what to say about it. The first thing that flashed in my mind was that out of all the thousands of people that they process I may have officially made it to the lunchroom conversation topic list of interesting characters. I do agree. It probably was not the sanest thing to say to a customs agent who is looking for suspicious characters, but honestly, I didn't think twice about it. It literally rolled off my tongue. I'm sure that was a channel message from spirit for content purposes!

He let me go through! I made it to the next gate, which was again delayed. They had to wait for the crew members to deboard from a different plane, so they had the necessary crew to get us back to Florida.

Finally in our seats on the plane, I asked spirit to please make the flight go by quick. I was way overdone for the day and needed to get home to my own bed. I had been awake for almost twenty-four hours at that point, and I was really tired. I'm pretty sure I fell asleep because I swear by the time the plane got off the ground they were saying prepare for landing. *Thank you, spirit!*

I retrieved my suitcase and went to the long-term parking tram waiting area. Once everyone loaded up, the driver went up and down every lane. It was almost midnight, and the majority of the patrons were older people who could not remember where their vehicles were. Some of them had little stickers that said what row or lane. They still couldn't remember where in the row or lane their car was parked. So, they proceeded to stand up on this moving bus using their key fob as we drove up and down aisles that were packed with holiday travelers, looking to see which car lit up.

I was sitting in the front of the bus, and the bus driver was getting grouchy. He grumbled, *"I get off in fifteen minutes and I still have to find a way to get the tram gassed up and I don't need this crap!"*

I was over-tired at this point and if somebody had looked at me the wrong way, I probably would've burst into tears. I was getting ready to just ask the gentleman to drop me off anywhere and I would personally walk the lanes just so I wouldn't inconvenience him.

Spirit flashed a visual to me that I had not had in a long time. I was instantly reeled back in thought to some boundary lessons I had already learned. I had also been reminded that this is part of his job. Spirit then showed me a fast-forward visual of what would have happened if I did get off the bus and sternly insisted that I was NOT to do this. So, I didn't.

Being the second-to-last person on the bus to be dropped off, the driver eventually got me to my car. I had taken a picture of where I had parked. Spirit must have made him feel bad for making *me* feel bad. He walked my suitcase to my trunk and even offered to load it into the car for me, which I let him do. He looked at me and said, "*I really do love older people. It's just been one of those days.*" I told him I understood and hoped his night got better.

Finally home, I took a welcome warm shower and fell fast asleep.

50

BACK TO HOGWARTS

The Arthur Findlay College,

Part 2: THE CLASS

Postcard

I want to dive into doing more mediumship readings for others. I do it without thinking most of the time, but I wanted to be in an immersive class setting for more practice to get more details. Can I do this already? YES! I think I just needed to go bye-bye. I knew it would be good for my soul.

Once I arrived it felt like a home away from home. I am officially an alumnus now, you know. I was given my room assignment in the mansion for this class. Getting to this room felt like I had tracked across three acres. I had never been to this area of the mansion. Actually, I didn't even know it existed. It was up and down four stairs here, three stairs there then around this corner, in a completely new area of the college for me where I had not been before. My room was a cozy corner with two windows and directly across from the bathroom.

I made fast friends with fellow classmates from the Netherlands, Australia, and New Zealand. We were by far the funniest, most jovial group of people in the class, and I could not have been more grateful. We all settled in quite nicely.

I was flattered that one of the main teachers actually recognized me. Trust me, *I was shocked.* It had been a few years and probably hundreds of students later. I was expecting to just blend in with the crowd, but I didn't. I would like to think it was because I made a positive impression the last time I was there. Or maybe it was because being the question queen that I am, possibly annoyed the pants off him and the other instructors.

This mediumship class I was doing was not for beginners. It was for people who were experienced. The class was called *The Way of the Medium.*

As we were all sorted and shuffled into specific groups, I had a chance to meet some very interesting fellow classmates from some of the far reaches of the globe.

There is one woman in our group who looked like Sinead O'Connor. She had a shaved head, was extremely nice and was understandable even though she didn't speak very good English. She was someone who had a small enough bottom that she could bring her knees to her chest having her entire body folded to be on the chair with room to spare. I admired this in her and had a new goal to aspire to! (Eventually.) That to me was talent!

The next standout person was Grey*. Grey is a super nice guy. Despite it being forty-two degrees Fahrenheit outside, Grey's daily signature clothing was a grey tank top, a pair of board shorts and Crocs, every-single-day. We were all cold looking at his clothing options, but it didn't bother *him* at all!

Then there was George*, a retired funeral director. This alone was fascinating for a million different reasons to me. Admit it! You have questions too! I knew if anyone was going to have some great stories, it was going to be him! On top of that he just turned seventy while in class and we sang "Happy Birthday" to him!

Those are just a few people at the beginning of the class. It was, and always will be, a reminder that doing this spiritual work does not have a signature look, style, age or attribute among us.

Given that it was after Thanksgiving but before Christmas, I got a chance to see the workers putting up the Christmas trees and decorations in the mansion. This made for some amazing backdrops for pictures!

Nothing about the college intimidated me going back like it did the first time. I had done so much more studying and work since having been there that I was comfortable and not intimidated. I knew what and how things worked already having done a tremendous number of readings!

In addition to the mediumship class that I was taking, there was also a spirit art class going on simultaneously in different parts of the college. We didn't interact with those people too much, but we still saw them at meals and coffee time.

Day 2

It's day two and I'm wondering if I made a mistake picking this course. *The Way of the Medium* is really not about the practices of mediumship but the other parts that you need to get in touch with to do this work. I was feeling like spirit did bait and switch on me! This is a touchy-feely, get-in-touch-with-your-emotions kind of thing. Of course, this is one of my weaker aspects, so I am up to my eyeballs in trying to adjust to this. I didn't feel like I did much of anything, but we did a lot of psychic work, which was good, because that seems to come very easy to me.

One of the things they discussed is that mediumship comes from love. You have to love yourself and honor the parts of you that come from love so that you can convey those messages to others. I feel my mediumship is not as fluid as I desire sometimes because of my own expectations. Spirit was basically telling me that if I don't see it in myself, I can't see it for other people. *Houston, we may have a problem.* DAMN IT!

I had quite a few people seeking me out, saying that I had such *good energy* and they wanted to work with me. I'm taking that as a big compliment. If nothing else, I'm a jokester and the giggly one. I kind of felt like one of the teachers was picking on me a little bit. Not in a bad way, but almost a fun, comedic type of banter. I was trying to keep it light and not go off the deep in defense at moments when a tender spot was poked.

During one exercise, I was paired up with a girl named Shelly*. She dressed sort of "grunge" and had a look that reminded me of the musician Joan Jett and the Blackhearts. I went first and got a contact for her. *I was aware of a woman who wasn't your mom or grandmother. She told me she is a friend. She is older than you. She wants you to know she's supporting you.* I asked Shelly if she could take any of what I was saying, and she said absolutely! I was getting my confirmation of goose bumps upside down and backward. I gave her the messages from this spirit and a bunch of other evidential information. It literally just rolled off my tongue.

When it was her turn to read for me, she told me that there was an older gentleman crouching down in front of me and she's seeing a stream and it's flowing gently but it's flowing. I feel like it was my grandpa, and the message was *let it flow, just go with it, I'm doing a great job and it's going to be fine.* I really appreciated the message from Shelly. I have come such a long way, but I want my mediumship to flow even more freely like a lot of well-known mediums. That is what I aspire to. But you guessed it, I have no patience.

As soon as the gift store was open, I had to go in and look and I saw two things that I really wanted to get for two friends here in

the States. They just spoke to me in such a profound way that

I immediately bought them and put them in my suitcase to give

as gifts.

There was one gentleman who was in our group, and he almost looked like he was forced to be there. Jack* was extremely vague about whatever you asked him. Like where he was from, what his story was and that he had a big secret he alluded to that he wasn't telling anyone about that explained his behavior. We're all digging in to figure out if he's really OK to be in the class or around people for that matter. He was there with his friend, the Sinead O'Connor lady. He just didn't seem happy. He almost had this black cloud of despair around him, but he wasn't divulging anything. He did admit he's got PTSD and there were a lot of traumatic events in his life and that he needed to get away from wherever he came from. Frankly it's kind of an odd excuse to take a mediumship class, but that is his story, and he is sticking to it. Luckily his energy is better today than it was yesterday.

Also, I would like to note it is forty-three degrees Fahrenheit outside and there are freaking mosquitoes. How do they survive in forty-degree weather? Inquiring minds need to know.

I had a really cool drop-in message for myself! I saw those deep red burgundy ropes that you will see at movie premieres, and they were gold ropes and red carpet. I don't know what that means. I'm marking it down!

Day 3

Something that I know about myself is that I like to go first during exchanges. I don't want any messages that are given to me to cloud or shadow the messages I give others. When I get messages from others and don't record them, I'm trying to remember, retain and analyze what somebody has told me first. Offering to go first, I could see the sigh of relief from other students who didn't want to be picked. There are actually a lot of shy mediums! I am definitely not one of them. It's something that I find works best for me because when I am receiving then I can just listen and let it marinate.

My great-aunt came through and gave lots of evidential information that the lady reading for me had but this overwhelming sense of love that I got from her message was awesome. I was shown that she was clapping her hands for me. She said I was doing great and that she loved me. It made me tear up. Often when spirit makes me feel love for the person I am giving a reading to, it is so overwhelmingly powerful and a beautiful feeling that I literally tear up. There is no other way to describe this.

Another one of my friends came through who fought a long and hard battle with breast cancer, and I knew it was her. Steph* has been giving me messages from the other side for a few years now. The people she has given me messages to pass on to are not ready to hear them yet, but she is not giving up. I am grateful and will always be a messenger for her when she needs me to be.

My friend and ex-sister-in-law, Dorothy, true to form, also came through. She always gives evidence, so I know that it is her. I was truly grateful. She follows me wherever I am and is a lot of fun still from the other side as a spirit. We had many years of history while she was alive and even more since she passed. She has helped me by tattling on many and has been a consummate cheerleader for me.

I did have a profound moment, because I finally had a chance to ask a question that I had been dying to know the answer to. You know they say, "*You don't always get what you want, but you get what you need,*" well I think this was one of those times.

When I am receiving information for others, I want as much information that I can process as fast as I can. I put myself in the receiver's seat. I would like to know and speak to my loved one who has crossed over.

As readers we don't know how long it will last or what will come through. This is how I feel about giving messages to people. I feel like I try to translate quickly and accurately as possible. I want to give as much information as I can. I don't know that this is bad at all but my guides know that I can process quickly and I am grateful for that.

During one of the teacher demonstrations for the evening, I watched one of the instructors get up and give evidence in the form of exact details specific to the person the message was for. He had finally narrowed it down to somebody in the group and what side of the room they were on. With further evidence, it was undoubtedly one particular person. There was one person (the sitter) who kept saying yes over and over again to the evidence. It was obvious that the teacher had the right spirit for the right person.

This went on for five to seven minutes. Just evidence. When the teacher asked if anyone had any questions my hand just shot right-the-hell up. My question was: *Why did you keep digging for evidence when you had the right person for the spirit that came through? It just seemed redundant.*

The answer was: *If the spirit wants to share the memory and talk about it—it's meant to share that memory with the sitter as no one else would understand. As a sitter they are just so grateful to finally have them around they don't care.*

This is not how I operate at all, but the theory of it actually made sense to me. I still feel that if a spirit makes the effort to come through it is to give a profound message, apologize, or show love, grace or support to the person listening. Again, I want that for the people I read for. I don't want to harp on about a teacup in a kitchen for five minutes and the person who came to me for the reading walks away with nothing. Anyway, that's how I feel. I want any sitter to walk away with as much as I can process and tell them.

There's a girl here from Brussels. I don't remember her name so we will just call her Brussels! She walks around like a church mouse. She's been to the college eight or nine times, but she doesn't participate. Her vibe is a cross between a church mouse and a nun. She smiles sweetly with her hands folded in front of her and she just walks around. Well, there's somebody in our group who was continually being paired up with her. This woman did personal one-on-one coaching as a profession. She finally had to go up to the instructors and ask that she not be paired up with her. She was there to learn and not work and it wasn't fair to her. Brussels would receive all the messages, but never would give any and that's not an equal exchange of energy.

After many conversations about this among us, we wondered if she was liking the attention because of her *lack of communication* with anybody. Just like some people and children. Negative attention is still attention.

It was the middle of the week. Like clockwork, everybody seemed to have hit the wall. Energy levels dipped to almost nothing. No one could keep their eyes open, and we all needed a nap. It's only for one day but boy, does the day drag! Something about this time is when the excitement and energy from getting there and getting settled has waned. We were all hitting the wall and couldn't seem to function. It just takes a bit more effort and a lot more coffee and tea.

We worked on color readings this evening. You were to intuitively take colors from a large open bin of crayons and colored pencils that represented the person you were paired up with. You color the forms on the paper you were given and then intuitively read for the person using just the color. It's surprisingly accurate actually. This was a fun activity and a change of pace. I will have to try this with my woo-woo group!

I took a few walks around the grounds for several minutes just to say hello to the trees, talk to my spirit guides, family and to ground. It was quite cold outside, and the grass was wet, so I stayed off the grass as much as possible. The last time I was out there was a few years prior. I was in tears pleading for help from my family on the other side to show me that I could really do this and was good enough. This time, there were no more tears. I wasn't upset or even frustrated. I was grateful. I felt like I had a firm grasp and understanding of giving and receiving messages so much more than what I had originally. I reminisced about the first time I had stepped foot on those grounds and being scared out of my gourd. I had come such a long way already!

One exercise that we did was to get in touch with our emotions. In front of the class without skipping a beat the teacher (also a psychology major) for this exercise looked at me and told me *I was going to have a hard time with this.* I thought it was kind of an odd thing to say to me. He really didn't know me. I remembered though, that I am in a room with empathic, psychic mediums. They can see and know things about you whether or not you admit them. I do this with other people. They can do it to me!

This exercise was to come up with three words to describe the other person intuitively. Then we are to lean into the words, feel what spirit means by them and receive messages for the other person. I was reminded by spirit that sometimes the statement that is given to me to give to another person may sound vague, but there's a reason. Spirit gives the message and we as readers need to dig into why they are bringing this up. Ask the spirit why it is important for the sitter to know and hear about it. I have to remember this because again, I'm so used to trying to get as many messages and information as I can that I could be missing some things.

I'm feeling like the messages I'm receiving from my fellow classmates have been more profound than the information I received from the teaching or course content. Of course, this could be me just with my head in the sand.

Day 4

I feel like the class is winding down. It seems like we're just doing filler exercises, and the bulk of what they wanted to teach us had already been administered. I have received and given a lot of messages but also my dreams have been crazy this week too I might add!

Some of the messages I have received have backed up other messages from readers in the States and also the channeling and automatic writings I have done for myself. It is always nice to get validation from across the pond. It makes you look twice at those messages.

There was a woman in our group, Trinity*. To me she was extremely beautiful and very fashionable. We paired up for one exercise. After she was done reading for me, she looked me in the eye and said if *I had my business up and running, I would hire you in a New York second and you have no idea how **powerful** you are*. Although I know I've heard those words before, I don't understand what they're saying because I am just me. I do what I do. It would be really nice if somebody would define what some of these things are that I do that make me powerful. I know I still have things I want to learn about. Maybe they are things I haven't learned yet?

Of course, one of the other things that I have been told is that I basically live a double life. There is the side of me that works with and helps other people and then there is the side of me that is just mom, Mimi, and businesswoman. I was warned that the time is coming to merge the two of them and it's probably going to be quicker than I think. *Gulp*

Day 5

It's the last day but it seems like the day kind of crawled by. We did our normal stuff, but I felt like some of this class was just to fill up space. Please understand something about me. I am like a sponge when I'm here. I am trying to get as much information as I can to learn and grow even more. I have an insatiable appetite for this stuff.

At one point they asked all of us in the group I was in to stand up in front of the class and say what we learned for the week. Also, to state where we are now in our learning, how are we going to take this information forward, and so on.

A lot of people were saying something extremely profound, and I honestly realized that I just needed to work on feeling more and not relying on as much psychic work. I channel quickly at moments. I need to slow up some and allow spirit to genuinely speak and give people the time they need when I'm getting the information. So that is what I said.

After, my group took a class photo on the stairs and then after dinner we were to report to one of the larger rooms for one last, final hurrah with the other group we did not practice with.

The chairs were all lined up in rows as a ceremonial type of situation. We all took a seat. There were a tremendous number of candles on one table to the left that were unlit and one large pillar candle at the front of the room that was lit.

After an opening statement, they asked each of us, one by one, to pick up a candle that had not been lit and light it from the pillar at the front. Then as you stand with your lit candle, to say what you feel is something you got out of the week. I knew we just did this in our group so I thought of something else I could say.

There were a lot of people in the room as there were two large groups merged. HOLY COW, somebody wore so much perfume that I think we probably could have choked to death, should somebody not have opened up a small window.

Each person got up and shared what they felt was very profound. A lot of people were emotional about what they said because it was very important for them for whatever personal reason. We all honored and respected where they were at.

When it was my turn, I simply said I had a sense of purpose. I know this is what I am meant to do. That's all I said. I put my lit candle on the table and sat back down by my friends again.

There was one gentleman who stood in front of everybody and said absolutely nothing. He literally just stared at the class in general. I'm not sure what that meant but as long as he did, that's all that mattered. I think he was probably just sending out energy, but he had this awful scowl on his face that was hard to interpret.

Brussels, the church mouse, never got up to say anything because she didn't want to. She just smiled politely and shook her head no. They skipped her.

Jack, the man who had PTSD and was super vague, said that he was very grateful for the week. His energy had shifted, and he felt he had found peace. He was definitely much more talkative and engaging than he was at the beginning of the week. We welcomed him with open arms and had many conversations with him during our free time.

Then there was Shelly, the Joan Jett grunge lady. She stood up in front of the class and said *I'm very grateful because I wasn't actually supposed to be here.* Of course, we're all thinking that she had a mismatched trip, or something happened. Then she further stated that *she had attempted to end her life a few weeks prior. It was unsuccessful, and through the grace of God and everybody around her they got her to this school. She was glad that she was alive.* I'm telling you what, we could not pass the box of tissues around fast enough.

Some of us were ugly crying! **There was not a dry eye in the room**. It was truly another complete validation that you do not know what somebody's going through and to just be kind.

On the flip side Grey wore pants to the ceremony with his tank top and Crocs. I'm not sure if he was finally cold enough to or if he ran out of shorts. Although I joke, he has quite a gift reading for others, and I enjoyed speaking with him.

Some of us gave hugs and said our goodbyes as we had early morning flights. Some of us exchanged business cards and did impromptu readings for each other in the lounge, which was fun.

I was honored, because as everybody was leaving for the evening and packing up their suitcases, the main teacher sought me out to say thanks for attending another class and it was really great to see me. I was so honored that he actually made a point to seek me out to make sure that he could give me a hug and say goodbye.

I feel like there's a lot that I need to digest about the week. If I could say anything about this class in general is that *I didn't get what I wanted but I got what I needed.*

I know mediumship. That's not the problem. It's being more in touch and honoring feelings of the spirit to convey to the sitter. I don't need to be a machine. I need to feel more into it to further honor the person who is sitting in front of me needing and wanting a connection with their loved one again.

I did learn some things I didn't think about. How about that?

I told everyone that the advantage of going home right now is that we were all going home with Christmas in just a few short weeks.

Hopefully everyone had fun events to attend. I know the week will be forgotten, but the memory will be burned in my brain along with the trip getting here.

I am so grateful for the assistance of the spirit world that came through for me. Of course, it was the help of my grandparents, great-aunt and friends. All the spirits were instrumental to me, and I love the messages that they gave to others and to me.

51

MY GRANDPA IN SPIRIT IS MAKING MORE FRIENDS

One of my good friends, Claire*, had just finished reading my first book, *SPIRITUALLY WAKING UP: You (Seriously) Can't Make This Sh*t Up*, and asked me if I wanted to meet over a glass of wine. I said of course! She then mentioned she had a message to give to me. Honestly, she had me at *let's meet for a glass of wine!*

When we met, she asked me to sign her copy of my book. I was flattered! Then she said, *Lisa, I must tell you, your grandfather came to me. I have some messages for you and then I have a question.* Claire has her own woo-woo powers and is working on developing them further. I'm always encouraging and helpful in answering questions or giving an interpretation for what she might get. Every so often she will have pop-in messages for me when we get together. But my grandfather in spirit was visiting her? What's up with that? I was intrigued.

We ordered appetizers and sipped on our wine chatting about various work and personal events. She then mentioned that my grandfather came to her and was talking to her. She said she felt she knew him from reading my book. I assured her that he probably *was* speaking to her. He has gone to my other woo-woo friends and urged them to pass messages to me many times before. Believe it or not, this didn't seem too unusual. Claire said, *Lisa, I sat up in bed and I swear to you he was talking to me! He was giving me messages and then kept talking about a flower that I'm supposed to get you.*

OK, now I am intrigued. Then she told me about the flower. She felt the message was that she was supposed to buy this specific flower for me. So before meeting me, she had stopped at three different floral shops looking for this particular flower. My grandfather told her that it had to be this specific color. She went on to say that none of the floral shops had this particular flower at all. She thought it was odd.

OK, WOW. I didn't expect this! This is a specific flower and color that my true soulmate will give me. That will be one of the telltale signs that it is indeed him. I was second-guessing myself that I might have slipped up and put this information in the book somewhere. With this information though, my head was swimming. It wasn't from the wine either! Why did my grandfather tell her about the flower and color? Why did she feel the need to go and buy me this? How else could that message she received be interpreted?

I validated what she said and told her that the flower means something to me. Somebody specific was to give me this kind and color of flower in the future. I also told her that there was probably a reason she couldn't find the flower. I explained that if she had, I would have to question a few things. She understood what I was saying and laughed and said, "*Maybe that's why I couldn't find the flower!*" I said exactly!

We laughed and then she gave me the other messages that my grandfather had given her to tell me. She kept saying that he was so nice to her and *funny*! I totally agreed with her. My grandpa and spirit team indeed are hilarious and fun.

Then she got serious for a moment. She said she didn't think about it before but, "*If talking to me while I'm in my room, can he see things?*" Oh, I knew what she was talking about! (wink, wink) I started laughing and told her I didn't think so. He can only see energy but it's interesting to think about, isn't it? She relaxed a bit and said, "*Oh yeah!*"

Anyway, she talked about a few different messages for me. I haven't been tapping in lately. When I don't, my spirit team will go through my woo-woo friends around me. Obviously, this was one of those times.

I was extremely grateful for those messages, too. I get a kick out of the fact that my grandfather is going to all the open people around me to give me the messages and makes more friends along the way. He is such a little stinker, but I applaud his energy and effort in a big way!

We had a good laugh over it all.

52

SPIRITS CALL FROM THE RED PHONE

I've been working diligently on a few projects nonstop. I found myself needing the assistance of someone to tweak my efforts further and they weren't available to help me at the moment.

I felt at a standstill. Even with my impatience, I had an odd feeling that came over me. Intuitively I felt that I just needed to chill out because there was a reason. This was new to me. I didn't know what the reason was. It was weird because why stop when there was a deadline? I am learning about listening to my intuition more and more.

Shortly thereafter though, I got a text from a woo-woo friend saying that spirit popped my name into her mind two or three times already for the day and I obviously needed a reading. I thought this was interesting because I knew there was a reason for the stall, but this time, I felt like I was being called to the principal's office. It was like I had to stop, put my pencil down, and report somewhere for a talking-to. I scheduled the reading for the next day.

I wasn't quite sure what exactly I was going to be told but to make sure that I stayed on task, I wrote down subjects that I needed clarification on. Hey, wouldn't you if you had spirit on the phone?

Before going to bed I asked spirit to get me up early since I had a scheduled automatic writing to do for someone. I also wanted to make sure it was done before I was given the reading by my friend. I ended up going to bed around 11 p.m. but woke up at 2 a.m. and could not go back to sleep until close to 5 a.m. *Spirit, this was not what I had in mind about getting me up early!* There wasn't anything too pressing on my brain that would keep me awake. The only thing was trying to figure out why I was being called to get a reading so randomly. In the past it's usually because I've got something pressing that I can't figure out, but I felt like I was on point doing everything I was supposed to be doing. I was looking on the brighter side thinking maybe it was good news.

I sat down to do my automatic writing for my client. As my hand began to flow on the paper, I was questioning if what was being said was for them or myself. There were so many similarities to what was going on in my life, yet this was somebody else's writing.

I marked that on my list of questions to ask spirit through my friend. There are quite often similarities between my life events and other patrons' lives at times. I get immense validation from these people through what spirit speaks to them about. This makes me think that before we got here how many of us picked the same life-experience package.

It was time for my reading. It was great to chat with my friend. I had not seen her for a bit as our schedules had not lined up for practice recently.

I told her I felt like I was being called to the principal's office, and we both laughed. I told her of a few projects I was working on and how there was a stall. Then she randomly contacted me to do the reading and I was excited to hear what spirit had to say because there was an obvious reason. If you don't think spirit knows what is going on without you telling them, think again.

My friend was telling me how the messages in her downloads she was receiving were for me. We both joked that when she gets messages for me specifically that they always seem to be in a metaphoric type of explanation. Not exactly black or white, just a roundabout way of saying something. I had given thought to this because this is true.

I receive messages for other people in the same manner. I know it will make sense to them, so I just repeat what I am being told to say. Here I was receiving messages for myself in the same way I give them to others. Fun stuff!

There were things like playing tic-tac-toe and how I need to be more strategic when I am playing. Then there was somebody in my energetic field that was like gum in my hair. I know these may sound like very crazy metaphors but believe it or not, they made sense to me.

There was also something said regarding dice and predictive qualities they wanted me to work on further. This was actually one of my strong suits when I participated in the ESP games at the Rhine (*www.Rhine.org*) a few years ago. There were multiple tests given to groups of us to test our abilities in remote viewing, psychic work, energy, and predictive abilities to name a few. So, I've got my work cut out for me. The reading did answer some of the questions that I had and clarified others.

It was a great reading. Of course, I recorded it because despite all the other messages that were given to me, my brain was still thinking about the tic-tac-toe analogy.

I find it interesting and yet intriguing that everything was put on pause because I needed to reevaluate a few things. The question I asked about the automatic writings was that they were indeed at times duly meant for me as well as for the client. Note taken!

We exchanged a bunch of stories and caught up on a few things before parting ways.

I told her how much I appreciated her, paying attention to spirit and stepping forward to allow me to receive a reading.

In a way I realized that I actually did have some questions that I was not vocalizing but internalizing. After we were done spirit made me aware of how much better I felt just talking out a few things and not internalizing so much. Yes, I spend plenty of time writing, but sometimes you just need a human being to bounce things off from time to time.

Anyway, I didn't get in trouble at the principal's office.

Now to get the energetic gum out of my hair, so I can play a better game of tic-tac-toe.

53

A Christmas Cheer Bully, Who Me?

I was reminiscing with two different friends this past Christmas over coffee. Their memories included me being a Christmas cheer bully. Yup! That sounds like me. I forgot about doing it though. I obviously had a forced cheer-up campaign in place for their Christmas holiday and in doing so made it to their personal history book! It's funny how things stand out to different people. I was just being me, but it made an impression on them they won't forget.

I want to stress that neither one of my friends were mad at me about my efforts. They just reminded me of my antics and tactics to make them feel happier against their will and how it worked.

The first friend I will call Jenna*. Jenna had a lot of personal stuff going on. She's always got a million stories to share and I love listening to her.

She had given me a key to her house at one point before going out of town and said that if for some reason there was an emergency that I could let myself in to help her if needed. I said OK.

Well here comes Christmas and I am in a really good mood. I asked her when she was going to put her Christmas tree up for which she couldn't give me a definitive answer. She was under a lot of stress and was going out of town for a few days. I was not having it and reminded her that I had a key to her house, and she had two choices. She could voluntarily get her stuff out and put it up by herself or while she was gone, I would use my key, let myself in, put a complete tree up and decorate the house, and she would have no choice. She looked like a deer in headlights. We negotiated. She said, *"Fine, I'll put it up, but you have to come over and help me,"* which I did. For every three Christmas balls we put on the tree, the cats actively swatted two to four of them off. We laughed as they bounced across the floor.

Jenna recalled this memory fondly. She said, *"Oh I'm not ever going to mess with you. You're going to come over and do it for me if I don't do it myself."* I had to laugh at how she relayed the story to me. She exclaimed that was one of the best Christmases, because I made sure that she was doing things that made her happy despite the circumstances around her. I had helped her shift her energy without even knowing it.

The second instance was with my friend Tina*. Tina and I needed to catch up as I had not seen her since moving back from North Carolina. During that conversation she brought up the memory that many years prior, I told her that she **had** to put a

Christmas tree up. She had some very tough situations going on at that time in her life. At the time she was newly divorced, and her father had passed away in the same few months. I just wanted her to be happy and she simply wasn't having any of it.

I insisted that she not wallow in despair but create new memories. Tina said that I offered to come over to her new place and put a tree up for her by myself and all she had to do was point and watch. She was shocked that I was going to do that, but after some contemplation, she agreed to decorate if I came over to help her. She said she would have hot cocoa if I was going to insist, and I did. She said she appreciated that I came over and helped her decorate and get her into the spirit. She said she would never forget how I pushed my way in to make her happy.

Funny how spirit uses you in certain ways to make sure that people get out of their own way. I had no idea about anything that I was doing or what was going on spiritually at that time. All I know is that I was happy dammit and everybody else had to be happy too.

There are no coincidences. I found it extremely funny that this Christmas these two particular people during the same season reminded me that I was a Christmas cheer bully and how grateful they were for it.

I can see myself doing this again in the future. I think I need a specific outfit for it though! I'm going to wear that title with pride!

Dear Reader,

I believe that my angels brought this up as a reminder that it's often the little things we do or say that are indeed more effective than we know. Although at the time your efforts might not be immediately acknowledged, they are remembered and appreciated. Always be kind.

54

YOUR OFFICIAL SPIRITUAL CHEAT SHEET

Want a cheat sheet? Well, here you go. These are some of the lessons I have learned on this awakening journey so far. They just matter. You may have more to add to this as you progress.

These are in no specific order or importance:

- Read everything you can get your hands on. Watch what you can. Listen to the experiences of others. Watch YouTube videos. Find books, seminars, and audiobooks. GET EDUCATED on narcissistic abuse as well as other personality disorders that might apply to your situation. The more you learn, the more you grow. *When the student is ready the teacher will appear.* Education will be your backbone to start. USE IT! YOU ARE NOT ALONE!

- Few will understand your journey and it is OK! Don't accept the labels they put on you because you are learning. Be OK with all of this.

- This journey can be lonely at times. Remind yourself that there is a difference between being alone and lonely. I have been in a room full of people and have felt alone. I have been alone and not felt lonely. Learn to love your own company. Know the difference!

- Know what trauma responses are. It might explain a few things about yourself and others.

- Regarding your spiritual gifts—just because you have the ability to "tap in and help others" does not mean you get a free pass from spiritual lessons. Just give that idea up!

- Doing shadow work will help you understand from the inside out what needs to be acknowledged, understood and corrected. It is not easy to rip internal Band-Aids off. It is messy and hard. Have tissues handy. Do one thing at a time.

- Don't compare your journey to anybody else. Even the most well-behaved, perfect-looking, nothing-ever-is-wrong people have a secret, a story, dark history, or some trauma behind them. Even if they look you in the eyes and try to convince you otherwise there is something. It just means they have yet to acknowledge them. No one, and I mean NO ONE, is perfect. Realize this and you see people differently.

- Forgive yourself! Give yourself a break for not knowing everything. You did the best that you could with what you had and where you were. It starts with you.

- Any attempt at a cram session or all-nighter, to get through doing shadow work to move on is a waste of time. Trust me, I TRIED. The faster you want to move, the slower spirit will force you to be. No matter how uncomfortable you get, you will be forced to sit in your feelings. You sit until it is no longer uncomfortable. It stinks while you're doing it but there is a reason.

- Faking the work to the outside world won't cut it. You can swear that you did enough but if spirit doesn't think so, you are doing it again! It will be new players but the same scenarios. Maybe the next time you will fix what truly needed to be fixed. I suggest doing it right the first time. Dig deep, go hard, get messy, and clear it up!

- If somebody does not want to get fixed, they are not going to be fixed. There is not enough love, effort, or explanation to fix someone else. You can only fix you. Your only job is to fix YOU. Not anyone else. Put the energy into you! No one else is!

- Practice receiving more. Learn what an equal exchange of energy is and own it. Stop giving so much time and effort to people that never give back to you. You deserve your share!

- Do not be somebody's life raft who just wants to see you drown with them. Misery loves company.

- Spirituality is not a cakewalk. It is not consistent rainbows, butterflies, or unicorns. Your light attracts some very unsavory people and circumstances. Learn to be aware and protect yourself. You can stand in the light or stay in the dark. You get to decide.

- Guess what? IF YOU DON'T FIX THIS STUFF NOW, YOU GET TO BE REBORN AND DO IT ALL AGAIN! If that doesn't sound like fun to you, I suggest getting to work!

- Your job is to make your soul happy and free again. If you want to know what a happy version of your soul looks like, go back through your pictures. You will see what true happiness looks like through your own eyes from an objective point of view. If you can't see it, ask a close friend. They will show you! Figure out why.

- If you feel like you are down and can't seem to find your happy place, put your hand over your heart and ask your soul what it needs to be happy for the day. Start with just one thing. THEN DO IT. It could be as simple as getting your crayons out and coloring. JUST DO IT!

- No one owns you. I have yet to hear of or see any baby being born with a manifesto stating that if so-and-so wants something you are obligated to give it to them. Don't let anyone control you. You have free will. If they still try, ask them to show you their paperwork, giving them that right. Bet they don't have it!

- Listen to your body and intuition. If it doesn't feel right, whether someone tries to convince you otherwise, DON'T. Just don't!

- The only way out is through. Even if you say you have learned a lesson, you still must walk through the fire. There is no shortcut. You can swear upside-down, backward, and twice on Tuesday that you're never going to do something EVER AGAIN, and you will STILL be required to walk through the fire.

- Fire hurts. It is to "gift you" a measure of pain and understanding so if you ever slap those damn rose-colored glasses on in the future, the pain, lessons, and fear of going through all this again will far outweigh the desire. Frankly, these sucks. It is necessary but it truly sucks.

- The work is unique to you, your circumstances, and your life. It starts with being self-aware. You have to start somewhere. Pick a place and just start. The lessons you need to learn will show themselves. There is no right or wrong. One thing will lead to another.

- No matter who you know or how you know, you cannot take a shortcut in your life. Think you did? Mark my words, it's coming back around.

- No matter who you talk to and what you find out, there are normally unseen twists and turns you could never expect. I-HAVE-TRIED. Sadly, more than I care to admit. Spirit will not let you cheat!

- Intuitive and psychic readings give you a lot of potential scenarios and helpful hints. They are not exact. They are at best, a guide. Only on occasion will a specific storyline actually play out. You have free will. Don't lean on them for all the answers. Look within, trust, and breathe.

- One thing leads to another. You are never fully done until you die. There are always loose ends to tie up.

- The baton of ancestral wounds will be passed on to generations below you until you have learned lessons. If you wouldn't wish your children or grandchildren to deal with what you did, fix it NOW. Lessons to learn are gifted generation to generation until they are stopped. BE THE ONE WHO STOPS THE MADNESS!

- There is always a carrot in front of you. Three more months, two more months, one more year, six more days, three summers from now. There's always another freakin' carrot. You're never ever done! Again, there is no finish line.

- If you watch closely and pay attention, spirit will remove experiences, people, places, and situations without you knowing, when they need to be. Seriously, POOF! They are just gone. Their part in your story is finished. Sometimes, you look for evidence of their existence and there is none. You will only know this by looking back. Don't spend that much time doing it. It's just for reference.

- Life is like a play. Everybody has a certain part to play in your life, good, bad, or indifferent. Some are there as lessons, some as blessings, some as guides. No one has a script. You are also a part in someone else's play. When each of your parts is done, everyone exits.

- You're not supposed to live for and worry about tomorrow. You're supposed to be present. Right here, right now. Be grateful for where you are. Practice being present.

- EVER-Y-ONE WEARS A MASK! We are all made of different layers of good and bad experiences and trauma. It's what makes all of us different and unique. We put on a different front for the different people we talk to. You truly don't know someone. Hell, you don't even know yourself most times! Work on yourself!

- Pay attention to your triggers. When you can tell your story and the lessons you learned from it without being upset, you are making headway. If something someone says or does, or a circumstance, causes a reaction out of you, lean into it and figure out why. That's what a trigger looks like.

- There are times when you will feel beaten down, spent, and thoroughly exhausted emotionally. You are so depleted you want to give up—DON'T. You deserve an amazing life and until you stand up and fight for it, you will continue to feel like this. If you do, IT'S A TRIGGER. Find the *why*! Show up!

- Some people portray that they have a cake life. They are hiding something. Whatever it is, it's NONE OF YOUR BUSINESS. Worry about yourself. You're looking at others to avoid looking at your own life. STOP!

- Your ONLY job is YOU. If you find you're trying to immerse yourself in other people's drama or situations, figure out why. This is a clear indication of you keeping attention off of yourself and onto others to avoid finger-pointing. This tactic you have says a lot about you whether or not you realize it. Figure it out. Dig deep and FIND YOUR WHY!

- You can't judge your journey by somebody else's. It is not a race. No one is getting out alive anyway. You are unique and will help people and the world in ways others cannot. Do not fret. YOU COUNT!

- This journey is a lot of UN-learning things that were pushed on you to conform. Be aware of this. It's a major head start.

- Spend time in nature. Trees and grass don't judge, and they are great listeners too!

- Realize if you are being pressured to conform it is often to make someone ELSE comfortable instead of you. Don't let it happen. Have strong boundaries. Read what they are. PRACTICE. Be strong. BE YOU!

- Just because someone is mad or upset doesn't make them right. Stand in your truth and use your voice.

- Know that some of the most well-meaning people in your life are often the most toxic to you. You will need to walk away or cut people out you used to count on. You can't get to shore if they keep putting holes in your boat. Learn to be OK with this. You will make new friends.

- Be around people because you want to, not because you have to. Learn to be your own hero and best friend.

- Once you graduate from rose-colored glasses of the 3-D world to the 5-D, you will suddenly see what other people's wounds are even if they don't. This is fascinating! You suddenly see low self-worth, lack of boundaries, abuse, neglect, and mistreatment. Despite knowing this, it is *their* responsibility to acknowledge and fix it. Until THEY see it themselves, nothing will change. The job is theirs. It's a gift to be aware of it but not your job to do anything about. Stick to the plan: YOU.

- Despite doing the work, no one is an expert. We all just have examples of our life experiences to share in hopes it will help someone else. There is no official "HOW I DID IT" manual. Listen to others' stories and take the information with a grain of salt. There is a reason for what you heard whether now or in the future. You will just know when it applies to you.

- Your loved ones, family, and friends on the other side want to see you succeed. Some family, friends, and loved ones here, often in private, don't. Pay attention to red flags.

- Let your angels and spirit guides HELP YOU. Learn to work with them and you will see the magic they can do for you.

- Find a collective. Meet-up groups, local metaphysical shops, book clubs, and so on. Find ways to connect with other like-minded people also on a spiritual journey.

Support helps! Whatever your interest you will find or will lead you to other like-minded individuals.

- DON'T BAIL. You might start feeling better and want to get back to old ways because you feel empowered by what you now know. Try not to. You're not done. If you do the work right, you won't. Know the difference. You will know this because YOU change and going backward just doesn't feel right.

- Angels cannot help unless you ask. SO, ASK! There will be some things they cannot help with because it would be the easy way out. Know they help more than you ever even know. Things go on behind the scenes you will never know about. Remember to say thank you for these, too!

- Learn and create your own language with your spirit guides and angels. It's like having a direct line to the other side. You have no idea how much this will help you!

- If spirit removes someone from your life, know they heard and saw things you didn't. Appreciate it no matter how much it might hurt in the moment. Do NOT try to get them back! Closed doors must stay closed.

- There are magic and gifts you hold that you probably aren't aware of. Find them. Bring them out to the surface. Practice using them!

- Your story might be someone else's survival guide in the future. Remember this!

- STAND IN YOUR POWER. Be unapologetically you.

- This work is not all doom and gloom. There are many, if not more, amazing, uplifting parts to experience and be had. It's a magical place, full of hope and joy.

I realize that there are probably many, many more things I have missed but these are some of the more profound things for me on MY journey so far.

I hope you find peace.

EPILOGUE

My journey is far from over. In a way, spirit has cleared the bench so that I will be in position to surge forward again. There will be a new home, a new job, a new location, and a new man just to name a few. My arms are empty, and I am ready to receive.

I am heading back to Hogwarts to put some further skills in my tool belt, learning to do some psychic detective work, among other things.

They have told me that the third book in the Woo-Woo series is practically going to "write itself." Given how my journey is going, I can only imagine how this next chapter of my life is going to unfold.

I have been told by spirit that there are still some "experiences" I need to have and untold secrets that will be revealed to me that will shock my knickers off. I am to share this with others and am reminded that my experiences would be someone else's survival guide. The world itself is in turmoil, and I am to be calm in the storm. Watch for book 3 in the Woo-Woo series, coming soon.

Also check out book one in the series, *Spiritually Waking Up; You (SERIOUSLY) Can't Make This Sh*t Up!*

About the Author,

Lisa Ann

Lisa is a prolific writer and the author of her debut book Spiritually Waking Up: You (SERIOUSLY) Can't Make This Sh*t Up! and book two in her WOO WOO Series; Hiding in Plain Sight; Confessions of an Angel Messenger.

Journaling for more than four decades, she combined her love of writing with her sense of humor and unique spin on life events. Through this palpable spark, she transformed her journey into her personal memoir to help others also going through a spiritual awakening by writing blog entries to document the often-hilarious life events. Her relatable life and disposition shine through as she explores the importance of really getting to know yourself on a deeper level.

Through her personal unfolding she has studied with numerous mediums in the US and UK. She also attended Arthur Findlay College in England for mediumship/psychic studies. She is also a member of Rhine Research Center, at Duke University in North Carolina. Aside from her career in the real estate industry, she is also a professional psychic medium, speaker, teacher of spiritual arts, and is the former host of the podcast: MESSAGE DELIVERY! You Can't Make This Stuff Up!

Lisa spends her downtime with her family, grandchildren, and friends. She enjoys traveling, camping, scuba diving and other various adventures when she is not learning about more spiritual endeavors.

She hopes her raw and often humorous stories help you to better understand what you might also be going through so you can navigate and embrace it for your future.